D1882561

INDIAN ZOOLOGY

INDIAN ZOOLOGY

THOMAS PENNANT

GYAN

Published by

Gyan Publishing House
5, Ansari Road
Daryaganj, New Delhi-110002
Phone: 011-47034999, 9811692060
E-mail: books@gyanbooks.com

Distribution Network
gyanbooks.com
India, USA, Canada, UK, Australia, France

© Publisher

All rights reserved. No part of this work may be reproduced, stored, adapted, or transmitted in any form or by any means, electronic, mechanical, photocopying, micro-filming, recording or otherwise, or translated in any language, without the prior written permission of the copyright owner and the publisher.

ISBN: 978-81-212-8758-6 (PB)
First Published, 1790

2nd Impression 2023

Printed at: Gyan Press, Delhi.

The book is sold subject to the condition that it shall not, by way of trade or otherwise, be lent, resold, hired out, or otherwise circulated without the prior publisher's written consent.

INDIAN ZOOLOGY
Author: Thomas Pennant

INDIAN ZOOLOGY.

SECOND EDITION.

LONDON.

Printed by HENRY HUGHS, for ROBERT FAULDER.

MDCCXC.

ADVERTISEMENT.

THIS work, or rather fragment, was begun in the year 1769. The deſcriptive part fell to my ſhare: the expence of the plates was divided between Mr. BANKS, now Sir JOSEPH BANKS, *Baronet*; JOHN GIDEON LOTEN, Eſq; a governor in *Ceylon*; and myſelf. Twelve only were engraved and publiſhed: ſoon after which, the undertaking appeared ſo arduous that the deſign was given over. It would be injuſtice to Mr. LOTEN not to ſay, that the etchings are taken from his fine collection of drawings made in *India*: for he alleviated the cares of life with the delicious purſuits of the ſtudy of NATURE. I prevaled on my two friends to unite with me in preſenting the learned JOHN REINHOLD FORSTER with the plates. I alſo beſtowed on him three others, engraven at my own expence, before the work was dropped. These were never published in *England*; but when Dr. *Forster* left our island, he took the whole with him, and in 1781 printed, at *Halle*, in *Saxony*, an edition very highly improved, and translated into *Latin* and *German*. He prefixed to it a most elaborate lucubration *de* Finibus et Indole *Aëris*, *Soli*, *Marisque* INDICI; described the subjects of the three additional plates; and inserted, after the description of the fifteenth plate, a most learned dissertation on the genus of the BIRDS OF PARADISE, and on the PHOENIX. He added several notes; and at the end presented his readers with a *Faunula* of the quadrupeds and birds of the extensive region of INDIA and its islands.

The last year, Mr. *Robert Faulder*, of *New Bond-street*, bookseller, applied to me for permission to reprint this very imperfect performance. I consented; but advised him by all means to get the additions by Dr. *Forster* translated, and an improved *Faunula* to be formed from the best authorities which

which could be procured: but, having myſelf abjured all future publications, referred him for that labor to any gentlemen willing and able to do juſtice to the performance. I took the liberty of pointing out three friends, of indiſputable abilities, and of whoſe kind ſervices I had long and uſeful experience.

Dr. AIKIN, of *Yarmouth*, in *Norfolk*, with great chearfulneſs undertook the tranſlations: Mr. JOHN LATHAM, of *Dartford*, *Kent*, juſtly celebrated for extending the ſtudy of ORNITHOLOGY far beyond any naturaliſt of our days; and the Rev. Mr. HUGH DAVIES, rector of *Aber*, in *Caernarvonſhire*, underwent the taſk of arranging the very numerous ſubjects of the INDIAN FAUNULA. The more laborious part, relative to the Inſects, fell to the ſhare of Mr. LATHAM: the reſt to that of Mr. DAVIES. A more complete enumeration was never formed, conſidering the extent of the country; and the materials imported into our iſlands. Science has of late years found its way into our moſt diſtant poſſeſſions; and we gather its fruits: the *Faunula* is a ſufficient proof of the richneſs of the harveſt. Collectors at home, or in the diſtant *Indoſtan*, will find conſiderable benefit from this part of the work. It will direct their reſearches, or inſtruct them in the arrangement of the new acquiſitions. If my paſt labors can in any ſhape contribute in the leſt to the amuſement of the individual, or to the public in general, the reflection cannot fail beſtowing on me the moſt pleaſing ſenſation.

THOMAS PENNANT.

Downing, March 1, 1791.

CONTENTS.

CONTENTS.

INDIAN

INDIAN FAUNULA, p. 57.

PLATES.

AN
ESSAY
ON
INDIA,
ITS
BOUNDARIES, CLIMATE, SOIL, AND SEA.

Tranſlated from the *Latin* of JOHN REINHOLD FORSTER,
By JOHN AIKIN, M. D.

THE name of *India* is probably derived from *Hind*, or *Hindu*, the appellation of the people inhabiting it, which the *Spaniards* and *Portugueſe*, the firſt navigators to *India*, were accuſtomed to write *Gentu*. The *Greeks*, who penetrated through *Perſia* into *India*, received from the *Perſians* the name of *Hind*, as that of the nation; but they alſo improperly called *Indus*, the river named by the inhabitants *Sind* or *Sindo*. In a later age, the *Romans* termed the country, *India*, the people, *Indians*, but the river alſo, *Indus*; yet they were not unacquainted with the name of *Sindi*. The *Arabians* and *Perſians* again employed the names of *Sind*, and *Hind*, which occur frequently in their writings. After the *Portugueſe* began to navigate for the purpoſe of exploring new regions, many of them ſuſpected, that if they were to ſteer directly weſtward, they would at length arrive at the fartheſt iſlands in the vicinity of *India*; and becauſe they conceived theſe iſlands to lie *before thoſe Indian* regions *(ante illas)* they gave them, in the geographical charts made before the diſcovery of *America*, the name of *Antilles*; and that *India*, which they ſuppoſed ſituated behind the *Antilles*, they named the *Weſt Indies*, becauſe it might be reached by ſailing weſtward. Hence appears the reaſon why in our age the name of *Indies* is ſo widely extended.

THAT *India* whence the animals now to be deſcribed are taken, is *Eaſt India*. But even here there is much variation as to the countries to which this name is proper and peculiar. In the firſt place it is maintained, that *India* is only wherever the *Hindu* nation inhabits, or the country called by the *Perſians*, *Hindoſtan*, which is comprehended between the rivers *Sind* and *Ganges*, cloſed to the north by the ridge of *Imaus* or *Caucaſus*; and on the ſouth ſurrounded by the ocean; ſo that the whole peninſula on this ſide the *Ganges*, belongs to *Hindoſtan*.

BUT in a more extended ſenſe, the peninſula beyond the *Ganges* alſo is a part of *India*. And its limits are much more extenſive, if under this ſecond ſignification of *India* are reckoned all the iſlands of the *Indian* ſea, from the eaſt and north of *Madagaſcar*, as far as *New Holland*, and thence eaſtward to the *Philippine* iſlands, together with *New Guinea*; and it is principally with this meaning that the *Engliſh* and *Dutch* ſailors uſe the word *India*, and Mr. PENNANT ſeems to have adopted it in his account of the animals of *India*.

FROM what has been ſaid, it will be evident that a diſquiſition concerning the climate, ſoil, and ſeas of *India*, thus largely underſtood, will be a matter of much difficulty.

MOUNTAINS.

MOUNT *Imaus*, ariſing in the very borders of *Perſia*, and whoſe northern ridge ſeparates *India* from *Bokara* or *Bactria*, from *Caſhimire* or *Caſpatyrus*, from the kingdom of *Tibet*, and from the *Chineſe* province of *Yunan*, terminates at length in the kingdom of of *Tonquin*, and runs out into other branches. At the root of this mountain the temperature of the air is very various; for in the winter ſeaſon the country is buried in ſnow and froſt, not, however, for a long time. Thoſe ſummits alone from which the *Sind* and *Ganges* are principally fed, are covered with perpetual ſnow. Yet even the plain tract at the mouths of the *Ganges* is not entirely free from froſt during winter, ſince the inhabitants collect ice artificially prepared, for cooling liquors in the heat of ſummer, although *Fahrenheit*'s thermometer never ſinks below 42. But in the ſummer ſeaſon the inhabitants undergo the moſt intenſe heats, ariſing to the 114th, nay even to the 120th degree of *Fahrenheit*'s thermometer; ſo that men are ſcarcely able to breathe, plunge into water up to the chin, and aſcend the higher trees that they may inhale a ſomewhat cooler breeze; whilſt they whoſe occupations oblige them to endure the hot air abroad, not unfrequently fall ſuddenly dead. The birds too are often killed by the heat, while flying, or ſitting on trees, and fall to the ground. GREAT HEATS.

THEN, as the flat country is inundated about the ſolſtice by the ſwoln waters of the *Ganges*, which returning into their channel, leave many ſtagnant pools, the exhalations raiſed by the ſun's heat form a body of intenſely hot vapour, extremely noxious, ſo as to occaſion putrid fevers of the higheſt malignity, which frequently prove fatal within three hours.

LET us now paſs into the peninſula of *India* on this ſide the *Ganges*, and examine the nature of its climate and ſoil. This part of *India* is divided into two parts by the ridge of mountains called *Gatté*; and while ſummer reigns on one ſide, winter prevails on the other. This chiefly proceeds from the winds, which, from

from *October* to *April*, blow conſtantly from the north; and from *April* to *October*, from the ſouth. For the ſpace of ſome weeks before this change, there is generally ſcarcely any wind; but at the commencement of the change, ſuch tempeſts ariſe as to cauſe great damage to mariners. On the eaſtern ſide of the peninſula, called the coaſt of *Coromandel*, the ſky from *April* to *October* is conſtantly ſerene without a ſhower, but from *October* to *April* is the rainy ſeaſon. On the weſtern or *Malabar* coaſt, on the contrary, there is no rain from *October* to *April*, but very heavy rains fall from *May* to *September*. During the fair ſeaſon, intenſe heat infeſts the whole coaſt; but in the rainy ſeaſon, the temperature is at intervals more moderate, and at that time all the rivers ſwell, and their ſtreams are partly diſtributed through the fields for the purpoſe of fertiliſing them, and partly are received into ponds or great receptacles, where the water is preſerved with care, to be let into the fields at proper periods.

The region of *India* beyond the *Ganges* has nearly the ſame climate with the peninſula on this ſide; but it is particularly well watered by large rivers. Of theſe we ſhall firſt mention the *Bahramputter (Burrampooter)* which flows through the whole country of *Tibet*, from the very confines of *Caſhimire*, and, after it has croſſed the kingdom of *Aſſam*, enters that of *Bengal* at *Rangamatty*, and at length, juſt upon the coaſt of the *Indian* ſea, mixes its waters with thoſe of the *Ganges*, in an equally copious ſtream, and thus enters the ſea in a common channel. Next, the rivers *Ava*, *Pegu*, and *Tenaſſerim*, riſing in the *Tibet* mountains, after watering the kingdoms whoſe names they bear, enter the bay of *Bengal* on the weſtern ſide of the peninſula.

RIVERS.

The *Menam* and *Menam-kom*, or *Siam* and *Cambodia* rivers, flow

flow down from the mountains which part the province of *Yunnan* in *China*, from *India*. All the above rivers, the *Bahramputter* excepted, take their courſe through large vallies, encloſed on each ſide by ridges of hills. On the approach of the ſun to the tropic of *Cancer*, the ſnow on theſe mountains is diſſolved, and all theſe vallies are overflowed, like *Egypt* by the *Nile*. When the rivers return into their channel, the moiſtened countries are ſown chiefly with rice, which yields a very rich increaſe. The kingdoms of *Cochinchina*, and *Tonquin*, are bounded to the eaſt by the ſea, and to the weſt by a ridge of mountains ſeparating them from the kingdoms of *Cambodia*, and *Laos*. From this ridge many rivers deſcend, which, after they have watered the country for a ſhort tract, mingle with the ſea.

THE ſoil of all *India* hitherto deſcribed is rich; and, by the cultivation of the populous nations, which from the remoteſt ages have inhabited theſe regions, and addicted themſelves to agriculture, is rendered extremely fertile. And, by reaſon that ſo many nations, and ſuch various ſpecies of animals, have for ſuch a courſe of ages putrefied with the vegetables of this fruitful land, the ſoil, lixiviated with water and mixed with aſhes, affords to *Europe* a great quantity of nitre, the principal ingredient of its gunpowder. Rice is chiefly ſown in moiſt ſituations, and ſupplies theſe people, who live a *Pythagorean* life, with a food of eaſy preparation, and extremely cheap. There is another kind of rice, which grows even on the hills, and ſpares the cultivators the labor of watering. SOIL.

THE marſhes are covered with thick beds of reeds; and, near the mouths of the largeſt rivers, overgrown with impenetrable groves of mangles. Among the cultivated tracts, here and there MARSHES.

dry

dry ſpots are obſerved, covered with briars and thickets. The parts neglected by human culture are full of woods, which abound with the moſt beautiful and ſingular birds, eſpecially parrots, peacocks, pigeons, and others infinitely diverſified with the gayeſt and moſt varied plumage; together with herds of antelopes, tribes of monkeys, and numbers of lions and tygers. The elephant, and rhinoceros, alſo inhabit theſe foreſts, which ſcarcely ever loſe their leaves, but are always verdant, and perpetually loaded with fruits of one kind or another.

ISLANDS. NATURE wears a different form in the iſlands of the *Indian* ſea. But, that we may the better underſtand the nature of the climate, and the temperature of the atmoſphere, it will be of particular uſe to conſider the courſe of the winds which prevail in theſe ſeas. WINDS. Between both tropics the wind almoſt conſtantly blows from the eaſt; and at the equinoxes, about the line, the courſe of the wind is directly from eaſt to weſt. For the ſun in the day-time heats the air; and about noon, when it is vertical, the atmoſphere glows with heat, and therefore is rarefied; at the ſame time, the ſun, ſeeming rapidly to move from eaſt to weſt, on account of the diurnal revolution of the earth, cauſes noon ſucceſſively in different regions. Towards evening, when the ſun is in the weſt, the air from both ſides of the globe, as likewiſe from the eaſt, ruſhes towards the weſt, and follows the ſun, in order to balance the rarefaction of the heated atmoſphere: this current of air is the eaſt wind. The greater the diſtance from the equinoctial line in each hemiſphere, the more the wind inclines to the north or ſouth. Now, when the ſun arrives at the tropic of *Cancer*, the eaſt wind follows it; but the eaſt-north-eaſt and north-eaſt extend beyond the tropic of *Cancer* into the northern hemiſphere, whilst, on the contrary, the east-south-east, and south-east scarcely reach farther than the equinoctial line. And when the sun recedes to the tropic of *Capricorn*, the east wind follows it there too; but the east-north-east, and north-east scarcely reach beyond the line, rarely to the tropic; while the east-south-east, and south-east spread far into the southern hemisphere. These observations are generally true concerning the winds within the tropics, and especially in the great *Atlantic* and *Pacific* oceans.

Every where within the tropics, on approaching within three or four leagues of land, a breeze is met with blowing from sea to land, from nine in the morning to sun-set; and from land to sea, from about ten at night to sun-rise. These observations also hold in general with respect to the winds in the vicinity of lands within the tropics.

In the *Indian* sea, from *October* to *April*, the east-north-east, and north-north-east winds prevail as far as the line. But during the same season, from the line southwards to about the 14th degree, the west, west-south-west, and south-west are the prevailing winds; and beyond this space, the east-south-east, and south-east. From *April* to *October*, in the northern hemisphere, the west, west-south-west, and south-west winds reign: to the south of the equinoctial, as far as about the 12th degree, the east, and east-south-east; and beyond that point, the east-south-east, and south-east. These prevailing winds are by sailors termed the *Monsoons*; and from them some inferences may be drawn as to the temperature of the air. The winds which blow across great tracts of land heated by the sun's rays, acquire a great degree of heat; and the greater space they pass over, the more scorching they prove. But wherever winds blow over the sea, they are cooled by the evaporation of the water: hence all ſhores and iſlands, though ſituated under the hotteſt ſun, enjoy the benefit of temperate ſea breezes.

Origin of the Islands.

If we mean to conſider the nature of the ſoil in the *Indian* iſlands, we muſt attend to their two-fold form and origin. Some are lofty, and if of moderate ſize, they have generally a conical ſhape. On examination of the mountain and ſtrata in this caſe, it will preſently be obvious that the whole iſland has emerged from the bottom of the ſea through the force of ſubterranean fire; for all parts are full of volcanic remains. Actually burning mountains are likewiſe not uncommon in theſe iſlands. All the high iſlands which I have ſurveyed between the tropics, in the *Atlantic* and *Pacific* oceans, were found to contain *ſcoriæ*, eructated aſhes, and liquefied matter, the manifeſt veſtiges of inteſtine fires. And that the ſame takes place with regard to the iſlands of the *Indian* ſea, is rendered probable by ſo many volcanoes yet to be ſeen among them, by the teſtimony of various navigators and eye-witneſſes, and by the ſtones, evidently reſembling *ſcoriæ* and melted rock, brought from thence. It is wonderful that aſhes thrown up from volcanoes, and other ſcoriaceous matters comminuted and mixed with the earth, ſhould conſtitute a ſoil inferior to none in fertility; but it is certain that moſt plants thrive moſt luxuriantly in this ſoil, and that trees of all kinds grow in it to a ſtupendous magnitude.

There are within the tropics other iſlands, low, and little elevated above the ſurface of the ſea. All of this kind are the workmanſhip of zoophyte *vermes*, which raiſe on all ſides from the bottom of the ſea their manſions of a calcareous matter, whence at length are formed rocks and ſtony ſhallows very dangerous

gerous to navigators. Since for the moſt part eaſterly winds are frequent in theſe ſeas, theſe animalcules, as if actuated by inſtinct, endeavour to exclude the waves driven by the winds, by means of their ſtupendous works; and therefore, carrying on the artful ſtructure of their calcareous or ſtony habitations, they extend them in long arms, which at laſt unite in a circle, within which they include a portion of calm untroubled ſea. On the oppoſite or windward ſide, the waves continually throw up fragments of corals, which, accumulating by degrees, form a mound againſt the force of the billows, and on that part the ſea is rendered gradually ſhallower; whilſt on the other ſide, immediately under the arms raiſed by the zoophytes, the ſea is of aſtoniſhing depth; and not unfrequently a part of the work remains open, for the ingreſs and egreſs of the tide. In the coral banks themſelves, ſand is collected by the waves, which afford ſoil and aliment for the ſeeds of ſhore plants brought thither by the ſea; and theſe plants at length periſhing, gradually create and accumulate a vegetable mould. If by chance a cocoa-nut be carried by the ſea to theſe ſpots, it germinates, and grows into a tall tree, bearing and diſſeminating many nuts, ſome of which again germinating, ſoon form a palm-grove, affording ſhade to birds, and other animals, and ſupplying navigators, driven to the place by ſtreſs of weather, with a grateful food and liquor. The bay included within the arms conſtructed by the zoophytes is a receptacle for fiſhes which require a calm unagitated ſea, and thus another food from the animal kingdom is preſented to ſtrangers. The ſhallows, too, afford quiet and deſirable ſituations to *molluſcæ*, and ſhell-fiſh of all kinds, and contribute much towards ſupplying the inhabitants of the iſlands with a variety of food.

THE greater iſlands of the *Indian* ſea, *Ceylon*, *Borneo*, *Java*, *Sumatra*, *Celebes*, *Luçonia*, *Mindanao*, *Ceram*, *Gilolo*, *Waighen*, and the iſle of *Papua* or *New Guinea*, are all mountainous, and full of burning or extinguiſhed volcanoes. They are covered with evergreen woods and reed-grounds, luxuriant in various tropical fruits, productive of all kinds of ſpices, and of many drugs valuable in

USEFUL TREES, &c.

medicine and the arts, eſpecially *Camphor*, *Benzoin*, *Gamboge*, *Sanders*, the *Amomums*, *Coſtus*, *Zedoary*, *Galangal*, the *Peppers*, *Snakeroot*, *Dragons-blood*, and many others which need not here be enumerated. Theſe iſlands, enriched with ſo many and great advantages, are everywhere inhabited by various animals; their woods and thickets are thronged with innumerable birds; their ſeas abound in fiſhes of all kinds, the greateſt part of which have never been examined by naturaliſts; and what vaſt treaſures of ſhell-fiſh their ſhores, marine rocks, and the bottom of their ſeas contain, may be gathered from hence, that for at leſt a century that theſe ſeas have been frequented by *Europeans*, they have continually been offering ſomewhat new to the curioſity of men whoſe avarice or vanity has prompted them to collect ſuch ſtores from all parts. Nor are theſe regions deſtitute of inhabitants, differing from each other in colour, ſhape, manners, dreſs, religion, and language. For ſome tribes in the interior receſſes of the woods and mountains preſerve their antient ſavage ſtate, treat all ſtrangers as enemies, and devour the ſlain; others, adopting gentler manners, and formed to commerce, and even to ſubmiſſion, become daily more civilized.

THUS much, concerning the limits, climate, ſoil, and ſeas of *India*, I thought neceſſary to prefix, in order to render what follows more perſpicuous.

ON

ON THE

BIRDS OF PARADISE,

AND THE

PHŒNIX.

THE *Birds of Paradiſe* are a genus of birds ſcarcely as yet ſufficiently known to the ornithologiſts, becauſe few of them are imported into *Europe*, and thoſe, too, mutilated in their feet, wings, and other parts, or diſtorted by having a ſtick thruſt within their ſkins, and thus too much lengthened. No real naturaliſt ever had the fortune to ſee a live *Bird of Paradiſe*, or to have obſerved their manners and economy *; for they inhabit a region viſited by very few *Europeans*, ſince ſcarcely any but ſailors and merchants are permitted to penetrate into the remoteſt eaſt, the country of the *Paradiſe-birds*. The hiſtory of this genus is therefore ſtill full of falſities, or rather buried in ſuch darkneſs, that we can ſcarcely hope to gain more and truer information concerning them, till ſome perſon, by a journey into theſe parts, is

* Sir JOSEPH BANKS did me the favor of communicating the drawing of the common *Bird of Paradiſe*, brought alive to *England*, drawn from the life. T. P.

enabled,

enabled, by his own obſervations and experiments, to give the public ſome accounts more ample and exact than we hitherto poſſeſs.

It is moſt certain that theſe birds were never known to the antients; and whatever the *Egyptian* prieſts delivered concerning their *Phœnix*, has little agreement with the *Bird of Paradiſe*. But, that there may not be the leſt doubt remaining on theſe points, we ſhall collect what has been ſaid by the antients concerning the *Phœnix*, and, after the paſſages are brought in view, briefly examine them. *Herodotus*, the father of hiſtory, relates (l. ii. 73.) that the *Phœnix* is a bird of the ſhape and ſize of an eagle, decorated with gold-coloured and purple wings; but he frankly confeſſes that he had never ſeen the bird, but knew it only by its picture. *Pliny* (l. x. c. 2.) confirms that the *Phœnix* is of the ſize of an eagle, with the ſplendour of gold around his neck; the reſt of the body purple; having a blue tail ſpotted with roſe-colored feathers; combs adorning his face, and a creſt of feathers, his head. This was the antient opinion concerning the form and colours of the *Phœnix*; but the ſame *Pliny* relates from *Manilius*, that the converſion of the great year correſponds with the life of this bird, from which period the ſame courſe of ſeaſons, and poſition of the heavenly bodies, is renewed; and that this takes place about noon on the day that the ſun enters *Taurus*. *Horapollo* delivers the ſame notion reſpecting the *Phœnix*. "They (the *Egyptian* prieſts) meaning to ſignify the converſion of the great year, paint the *Phœnix*." Theſe notions are then to be explained from the theology of *Egypt*.

The *Sun*, which *produces the ſeaſons*, is the *Egyptian* Osiris, a deity whoſe name has the ſame ſignification; for *Oeiſch-iri* in the

Egyptian tongue, is the *maker of ſeaſons.* But almoſt all the male gods, eſpecially, of the *Egyptians,* expreſſed the virtues and powers of the Sun. Hence, the vernal ſun, when it is peculiarly vigorous, and operates with moſt power, according to the diſcipline of the *Egyptian* prieſts, was *Hercules,* whom they therefore called *Dſemmenuti,* the *virtue of God,* or *of the Gods.* The ſame *Hercules,* according to *Athenagoras (pro Chriſtianis,* p. 18.) or, as *Damaſcus* has it (περι αρχων ap. *Wolff. Anecdot.* iii. p. 254.) " that principle was named, *time void of old age,* and likewiſe *Hercules.*" Nor is it to be omitted, that in the obeliſk of king *Rameſſes,* the ſun is called *the lord of ſeaſons,* which in the *Egyptian* language is *Seſoeiſch,* or *Seſooſis.*

The annual revolution of the ſun makes a year of twelve months; but the *Egyptian* year, long, was only 365 days; whence, every fourth year, four true ſolar years exceeded as many *Egyptian* years a ſingle day, which they were not accuſtomed to intercalate. Hence the ſeaſons of the year wandered through the whole *Egyptian* year; and hence of the ſolar years as firſt fixed by *Julius Cæſar* the dictator, 1460 equal 1461 vague *Egyptian* years. On this account, the *Egyptian* prieſts were accuſtomed to call four years with the day of intercalation, *the year of God*; and 1461 vague *Egyptian* years made the *great year of God,* that is, of the *Sun.* And they taught, that at this great period, the *converſion of the great year* took place, at which alſo the *Phœnix* regenerated—flew from *Arabia* to the city of the ſun, and depoſited his father's body on the altar.

It will now appear, why the *Orphics,* in hymn xi. to *Hercules* 3. addreſs him by the title of *various-formed father of time.* And *Plutarch,* in his treatiſe on *Iſis* and *Oſiris,* aſſerts, " that the

the *Egyptians* fable *Hercules* to be placed in the ſun, and to revolve with it." For, from theſe premiſes, it might juſtly be ſaid, with *Nonnus of Panopolis*, l. xl. p. 683, " that *Hercules* rolls round the whole earth in the glittering orb of the ſun, and carries round with him the year, the ſon of time." Every common year, therefore, is a year of God; and the great year, the *ſon of time*, which, in the *Egyptian* language, would be *Dſphenoeiſch*, and, on account of the harſhneſs of the firſt letter, the *Greeks* would make it φοινιξ, *Phœnix*. This origin of the name adds ſtrength to my opinion, ſince it is perfectly agreeable to the doctrine of the *Egyptians* concerning theſe things, and at the ſame time exactly expreſſes all the ſacred fables of their prieſts relative to the *Phœnix*.

THAT the fabulous *Phœnix* of the *Egyptians* has nothing in common with the *Birds of Paradiſe*, will be ſufficiently manifeſt from what has been ſaid; yet it is not altogether without reaſon that we have here treated on the *Phœnix*; for the firſt *Portugueſe* navigators to the *Indian* iſlands called the *Birds of Paradiſe*, *paſſaros da ſol*, *Birds of the ſun*, in the ſame manner as the *Egyptians* had regarded the *Phœnix* as a ſymbol of the annual revolution of the ſun, and the converſion of the great year. The inhabitants of the iſle of *Ternate* call theſe birds *Manu-co-Dewata*; *Birds of God*. The *French*, *Engliſh*, and *Germans* have adopted the name of *Birds of Paradiſe*. All theſe names ſeem to attribute ſomewhat of a *celeſtial* origin to the birds. The name *Manu-co-Dewata* has induced ſome writers of natural hiſtory to call the bird *Manucodiata* (*Edwards*, t. 110. *Marcgrav. Braſil*, 207. *Raii Synopſ. Av.* 21. n. 7. *Briſſon Ornithol.* ii. p. 130.) and the illuſtrious count de *Buffon*, by cutting off part of the name, has made from it it his *Manucode*. *Valentyne* (vol. iii. p. 306, 313.) has treated at length of the *Birds of Paradiſe*. The *Portugueſe* firſt ſaw them in *Gilolo*, *Papua*, and *New Guinea*. Many idle fables have been propagated concerning theſe birds; among which are to be reckoned, that they have no feet, are always on the wing, paſs their lives in the air and feed on this element; on which account the inhabitants of theſe countries are accuſtomed to cut off their feet. But the people of the *Aru* iſlands have taught the *Dutch* in *Banda* better; and it is found that the feet are cut off in order that the birds may be more eaſily preſerved dry. The *Indians*, too, pay little regard to the feet, becauſe they uſe the ſkins of the *Birds of Paradiſe* only to adorn their helmets in their games and mock combats. But the *Aruans*, 70 or 80 years ago, brought theſe birds with their feet. *Pigafetta*, who accompanied *Ferdinand Magalhaens* in his voyage, teſtified from ocular demonſtration, about 1525, that they were not without feet. But the length and peculiar ſtructure of the ſcapular feathers, prevent them from ſitting on trees in windy weather; and if they are once blown down to the ground, they are utterly unable to raiſe themſelves again by their wings. When taken by the natives, they are immediately killed, becauſe their food is unknown, and they defend themſelves courageouſly with their very ſtrong beaks.

Of the *Birds of Paradiſe* there are about ſix ſpecies *.

1. The great *Paradiſe-bird* of *Aru*.
2. The leſſer *Paradiſe-bird* of *Papua*.
3. and 4. Two black ſpecies.

* The *Faunula* will produce many more.

5. The white *Paradiſe-bird.*

6. The unknown *Paradiſe-bird.*

7. The leſſer *King-bird,* which is alſo to be reckoned among the *Paradiſe-birds.*

I. Paradisæa apoda. Greater Bird of Paradise.
Latham Syn. ii. 474. *Index,* i. 194.

THE *greater Paradiſe-bird* is generally about two feet in length. Head, ſmall: beak, the length of the head, hard, pale-coloured. Head and nape of the neck, yellow. Space round the eyes, black. Neck, beautifully reſplendent with very ſoft, ſhining, emerald-coloured feathers: thoſe of the breaſt, equally ſoft, of a pale yellowiſh-grey. Large cheſnut-coloured wings. Back covered with the ſcapulars elongated, ſtiff, narrow, pale brown, very much reſembling the looſe feathers of the oſtrich. Theſe expand while the bird flies; and therefore it is eaſy for him to remain in the air. On the ſides of the breaſt and belly are bundles of feathers, much ſhorter than the anterior ones, ſtiff, gold-coloured. From the rump ariſe two ſtiff feathers of great length, naked in the ſhafts, terminated with radiated plumes. Several birds of theſe countries are furniſhed with ſuch long feathers, as the *Belurus (Pylſtaart)* of *Amboyna,* the *Alcedo Sariwak,* and a ſpecies of *Papuan* parroquet. In ſize it little exceeds the blackbird. Feet ſhort, with four ſtrong toes. The inhabitants of *Ternate* call this ſpecies *Burong Papua, Papua* birds; and ſometimes *Manu-co-dewata,* and alſo *Soffu,* or *Sioffu.* The *Amboyneſe* call them *Manu-key-aru,* birds of the iſlands *Key* and *Aru,* becauſe

because the people of these islands bring them to *Banda* and *Amboyna* for sale. The *Aruans* give them the name of *Fanaan*. In fact, these birds are not found in the island *Key*, which is about 50 miles eastward of *Banda*, but are met with in the *Aru* islands (which are 15 miles further to the east than *Key*) at the dry season of the western monsoon, and return to *New Guinea* at the commencement of the rainy season, as soon as the east wind begins to blow. They fly in flocks of about 30 or 40, led by a bird which the *Aruans* call KING, but which is altogether distinct from the lesser *Bird of Paradise*. This leader is black with red spots, and constantly flies higher than the rest, which never separate from it, but immediately when it settles, settle too; whence they frequently perish, for if the leader settles on the ground, they are not able to rise on account of the peculiar structure of their feathers. Nor can they fly with the wind, for in that case their very long loose feathers would be totally disordered: they therefore always fly against the wind, and carefully abstain from flight in a storm, which often throws them to the ground.

WHILE flying they are noisy, like starlings; but their cry rather resembles the croaking of ravens, and is particularly audible, when in windy weather the incumbrance of their feathers brings them into imminent danger of falling to the ground. In the *Aru* islands they perch on the highest trees, especially on those of the small-leaved *Waringha* with red fruit, on which they chiefly subsist (*Ficus Benjamina? Hort. Malab.* iii. f. 35. *Rumph. Amboin.* iii. f. 90.) They are taken by the inhabitants with bird-lime, snares, or blunt arrows. But though many fall alive into the fowlers hands, they are immediately killed, and after embowelling, and generally cutting off their feet, they are fumigated

 with

with ſulphur, and dried; in which ſtate they are ſold, for half a dollar in *Banda*, but in *Aru* they may be purchaſed for a large nail or piece of iron. The *Dutch* ſhips frequenting the ſea between *New Guinea* and *Aru* (a diſtance of 18 or 20 miles) not unfrequently ſee flocks of *Paradiſe-birds* croſſing the ſea from one to the other of theſe places, but always againſt the wind. If a more tempeſtuous gale than uſual riſes during their flight, they ſeek the upper and calmer regions of the air, and thus continue their courſe. The natives faſten theſe birds to their helmets in place of creſts, in real and mock fights; and often tie the whole or part of the ſkins to their ſwords. During the eaſtern monſoon their very long feathers fall; and in the weſtern monſoon, within the ſpace of four months, as the *Aruans* report, they are replaced by new ones.

II. Paradisea apoda. Lesser. *Latham Syn.* ii. 474. *Index*, i. 194. β.

THE leſſer Paradiſe-bird of Papua. This ſpecies is about twenty inches in length. Beak, lead-colored, paler towards the apex. Eyes, ſmall, and ſurrounded with black. Neck, emerald-colored. Head, and back of the neck, duſky-yellowiſh. Wings, ſmall and cheſnut-colored. Breaſt and belly, brown. Back, yellowiſh-grey. Long ſcapulars, about a foot in length, and paler than in the former ſpecies; which is in general to be obſerved of all the ſplendid colours in this ſpecies. The long bare feathers of the tail are conſtantly rejected by the inhabitants. In other reſpects, this ſpecies has every thing in common with the

3 former.

former. These birds also follow a leader; which, however, has more of a dark purple in his wings; but this leader is distinguished from the 3d and 4th black kinds. The *Papuan* inhabitants of the island *Missowal, (Mixoal, Maysol)* relate that these *Paradise-birds* never migrate, but build nests in the highest trees, where they are found by the *Alfubris*. The beak and neck are longer in the male than in the female. By the people of *Ternate*, and *Tidore*, this bird is called *Toffu* or *Burong Papuwa*, *Papua-bird*. By the *Papuans* it is named *Shag* or *Shague*. The people of *East Ceram* give it the name of *Samaleik*; but in the isle of *Serghile*, in *New Guinea*, it is called *Tshakke*. It was formerly believed that these birds were found in *Gilolo* or *Halamahera*, and the adjacent islands to the south and south-east; but it is now certain that they are peculiar to the *Papuan* isles. These extend from the southern extremity of *Gilolo*, and northern coast of *Ceram*, as far as the western part of *New Guinea*. The largest of them are *Missowal (Maysol)* lying to the north of *Ceram*; and *Salawatti*, or *Salawat*, situated near the country or island of *Serghile*, in *New Guinea*. This last, in the earliest *Portuguese* maps, is improperly called *Ceram*, and is separated from *New Guinea*. These *Paradise-birds* perch on the highest trees of the mountainous region, and are killed with blunt arrows by the people of *Missowal*. Others relate, that the natives medicate the water of which the birds are used to drink, with the *India*-berries *(Menispermum Cocculus Linn.)* whereby they are rendered so stupid as to be taken by the hand. These birds commonly feed on the fruit of the *Tshampeda*-tree, which they perforate with their bills, and thus extract the kernels. It is fabled by some, that when these birds become weak with age, they fly a great height towards the sun, fun, till they fall down dead. The *Papuans*, after killing and embowelling them, dry the cavity with a hot iron, and enclose them in a joint of *bamboo*, in order the better to preserve them.

III. and IV.

THE *black Paradise-birds*. The larger variety of these is sold by the natives without wings and feet, and therefore is very difficult to be described with accuracy. The remains are generally stretched out on a stick to the length of four spans. The feathers of the head, neck, and belly are black, silky, and mixed with a radiant hue of purple and gold. Beak, blackish, an inch long. From both sides spring bunches of feathers, somewhat similar to quill-feathers, but in reality very different from them, for this species is always offered to sale with the wings cut off. The feathers in these bunches are extremely soft, with broad webs like peacocks feathers, of a fine shining green, and all reverted; whence *Valentyne* suspects that they become reverted in the *bamboo* joints in which they are enclosed by the natives. Tail, wedge-shaped. Tail feathers next the abdomen, hairy; upper ones, longer, and pointed; those immediately beneath these, above a span and a half in length, stiff, with loose doubly compound rays, black above, shining below. The birds of this variety are brought only from the part of *New Guinea* called *Sergbile*. The inhabitants carry the skins dried upon sticks by smoke, and enclosed in bamboo joints, to the island *Salawat*, and exchange them for hatchets and coarse cloths. The *Papuans* call them *Shagawa*, and also, *Paradise-birds* from *Sergbile*: in *Ternate* and *Tidore*, they are called *Soffu-kokotu*, *Black Paradise-birds*.

birds. *Serghile* is the moſt northern part of *New Guinea*, running out to a ſharp promontory, ſituated beyond or to the eaſt of *Gilolo* and the *Papua* iſland, and facing the north.

Besides the *greater black Paradiſe-bird*, there is a *leſſer* variety. Its feathers are equally long, but not ſo thick; black above, not ſhining. This variety is alſo deſtitute of the ſhining peacock feathers found in the firſt. It likewiſe wants the three long pointed tail-feathers, which are proper to the greater kind. The *Alfubris*, or inhabitants of the mountainous part of the iſle of *Meſſowal*, ſhoot theſe birds with arrows, and ſell them to the people of *Tidore.*

V. Paradisea alba, *Latham Index*, i. 197.
β. Wayghihu. *The ſame.*

THE *white Paradiſe-bird* is the rareſt of all the ſpecies, and has two varieties, one entirely white, the other black and white. The firſt is very rare, and in habit much reſembles the *Paradiſe-bird* of *Papua*. The ſecond variety has its fore-part black, and back-part white, with twelve ſlender crooked almoſt naked feathers. This kind is the rareſt of all, and is procured only through the people of *Tidore*, becauſe it is found in thoſe *Papuan* iſles only which are little frequented, particularly in *Wayghibu* (called alſo *Wadju*, *Wardju*, and *Waygiu.*) Some ſuſpect that they are imported from *Serghile*, in *New Guinea.*

VI.

VI.

IN 1689, a new ſpecies of *black Paradiſe-bird* was firſt ſeen at *Amboyna*, brought from *Miſſowai*, about a foot in length, with a ſhining purpliſh hue. Head, middle-ſized; bill, ſtraight; back, as in the other ſpecies, adorned with purple-blue feathers, but under the wings, and on the belly, yellowiſh, as in the apodous ſpecies. Back of the neck, mouſe-colored, greeniſh. In this kind it is obſervable, that on the ſcapulæ are bundles of green-edged feathers, which can be erected at pleaſure, like wings. In place of a tail, it has twelve black, naked, ſetaceous and thready ſhafts, like pendulous feathers. Feet ſtrong, with ſharp claws. Head ſmall; eyes encircled with black.

VII. PARADISEA REGIA. KING. *Latham Syn.* ii. 475. *Index*, i. 194.

THE laſt ſpecies is the *King-bird*, which ſome reckon among the *Paradiſe-birds*; but, according to *Valentyne*, it is totally different from them. LINNÆUS and BUFFON, however, refer them to the *Paradiſe-birds*, chiefly induced by the ſhape of the bill, and the feathers peculiar to this genus. This bird is about ſeven inches in length, and ſomewhat exceeds a titmouſe in bulk. Head, and eyes (which are ſurrounded with a black circle) ſmall. Beak, ſtraight. Crown of the head, flame-colored: nape of the neck, blood-colored: neck and breaſt, cheſnut, with a band of bright emerald. Wings, large for the body; quill-feathers black, with rays ſpotted and ſtreaked with ſhining red. Tail, ſtraight, ſhort, and brown. Intermediate tail-feathers, long, thread-

thread-ſhaped, black, exceeding the reſt a palm in length, with a lunated feathered tip, of a ſhining green above, brown below. Belly, ſpotted: from the ſides proceed bundles of broad-rayed feathers, one part of the rays, green, the other, brown. Back, blood-brown, gloſſy like ſilk. Feet, like thoſe of a lark; three toes before, one behind.

This bird never aſſociates with the other ſpecies of *Paradiſe-birds*, but flies about the lonely thickets, wherever it ſees red berries, nor ever ſits upon tall trees.

In *Aru* it is called *Wowi Wowi:* in the *Papua* iſles, *Sopclo-o.* The *Dutch* name it *Kings-bird.* It is chiefly brought from *Aru-Sopclo-o*; and eſpecially from *Wodjir*, a well-known town of this iſland. The *Aruans* ſay they have never ſeen its neſt; but ſuſpect that it is a ſtranger from *New Guinea*, and there brings up its young, but never leaves *Aru* during the dry ſeaſon of the weſtern monſoon. It is taken in ſnares made of *Gummatty*, or with birdlime prepared from the *Sukkom* or bread-fruit (Artocarpus communis *Forſt. Charact.)*

It is embowelled and dried, and ſold in *Banda.* The *Aruans* put it in their helmets in their mock fights, and the game *Tobakalil.*

The illuſtrious Buffon, or rather his friend *Gueneau de Montbeillard*, deſcribes ſix *Paradiſe-birds* in his Hiſt. of Birds, tom iii. edit. in 4to: and tom v. edit. in 12mo, p. 207, 238. Theſe birds ſeem alſo to be delineated in *Daubenton*'s ſplendid *Planches Enluminées*, N° 254, 496, 631, 632, 633, 634. *Sonnerat* likewiſe deſcribes and delineates the ſame ſix birds. We ſhall now therefore briefly compare theſe ſix birds with what we have above deſcribed at length from *Valentyn*, vol. iii.

 I. *L'oiſeau*

I. *L'oiseau de Paradis*, is *Valentyn*'s, 1. *Paradisea major Aruana*; and the *Paradisea apoda Linn.*

II. *Le Manucode*, is *Valentyn*'s, 7. *Avis regia*; *Paradisea regia Linn.*

III. MAGNIFICENT. *Latham Syn.* ii. 477. *Index*, i. 195.

Le Magnifique, ou Manucode à bouquets, may seem in some respects referable to *Valentyn*'s *Paradisea minor Papuana*; though I confess it much differs from it.

IV. SUPERB. *Latham Syn.* ii. 479. *Index*, i. 196.

Le Superbe, ou Manucode noir, as delineated in the *Planches Enlum.* seems to be either a young bird, or a hen, or taken at the moulting season; for *Valentyn*'s 3. *Paradisea nigra major*, has long setaceous feathers in the tail; and the Hist. of Birds, as well as *Daubenton*'s *Le Superbe*, are without them. What *Gueneau de Monbeillard* observes, however, is not to be overlooked; that the specimens in the royal *Paris* museum are ill kept, and have lost these long feathers by accident.

V. GOLD-BREASTED. *Latham Syn.* ii. 481. *Index*, i. 196.

Le Sifilet, ou Manucode à six filets. I can scarcely help thinking that this is *Valentyn*'s, 4. *Paradisea nigra minor*, which by chance or design had lost its long filaments near the ears.

VI. BLUE-GREEN. *Latham Syn.* ii. 482. *Index*, i. 197.

Le Calybé, seems to be an obscure species.

THE

THE other *Paradiſe-birds* of *Valentyn* are not yet ſufficiently aſcertained. It is greatly therefore to be wiſhed, that a naturaliſt ſhould undertake a journey into *New Guinea*, and the *Papua* iſles, ſince theſe regions ſeem full of new and unexplored natural wonders. In the meantime we hope that theſe obſervations concerning the *Birds of Paradiſe* will not be unacceptable to thoſe who are deſirous of an accurate knowledge of the works of Nature.

INDIAN ZOOLOGY.

Pl.

THE LONG TAILED SQUIRREL.

I.

SCIURUS MACROURUS.

THE LONG-TAILED SQUIRREL.

Sciurus *Zeylanicus* pilis in dorſo nigricantibus, *Raii Syn. Quad.* 215.
Sc. Macrourus, *Gmelin. Lin.* i. 148.

THIS ſpecies is found in *Ceylon* and *Malabar*. In the *Cingaleſe* tongue it is called *Dandoelana*; and, from the noiſe it makes, *Roekea*. LONG-TAILED SQUIRREL.

IT is about three times the ſize of the *European* ſquirrel.

THE ears are tufted with black hairs: the end of the noſe is pink-coloured: the cheeks, legs, and belly, are of a dull yellow: between the ears is a yellow ſpot: the crown of the head, and the back, are black: from each ear is a bifurcated line of the ſame color, pointing down the cheeks: the upper part of the feet is covered with black hairs: the lower part naked and red.

THE tail is near twice the length of the body, of a light aſh-color, and extremely buſhy. The part next the body quite ſurrounded with hairs: on the remainder the hairs are ſeparated, and lie flat.

THE.

EUGENIA MALAC.

THE tree is the JAMBU *Rumph. Amboin.* i. 121. *tab.* 37. EUGENIA MALACCENSIS, *Sp. Pl.* 672. *Fl. Zeyl.* N° 187. It is the moſt excellent of the *Indian* fruits, delicious in taſte, grateful in ſmell, pleaſing to the eye, and ſalubrious in its effects.

ITS native place is *Malacca*; and is only cultivated in *Goa* and *Amboina*, on account of its fine qualities, its roſeate ſcent and color, and its happy faculty of allaying the rage of thirſt in the burning fevers of the torrid zone.

P. II.

THE BLACK & WHITE FALCON.

II.

FALCO MELANOLEUCOS.

BLACK AND WHITE FALCON.

F. Melanoleucos, *Gmelin. Lin.* i. 274. *Latham*, i. 81. *Index Ornith.* i. 36.

INHABITS *Ceylon*: its length is fixteen inches, its weight about ten ounces. BLACK AND WHITE FALCON.

THE bill is black: the irides of a reddifh yellow: the orbits marked with white fpecks. The head, neck, back, fcapulars, quil-feathers, and fome of the middle coverts of the wings, are black; the reft of the coverts, thofe of the tail, the tail itfelf, the breaft and belly, are of a pure white.

THIS fpecies is called in the *Cingalefe*, *Kaloé Koeroel-goya*. We are uncertain whether it is trained for the amufement of falconry, as fome other kinds are, by the natives of *Ceylon*.

THE tree is the *Vidara* of *Rumphius*, ii. 17. *tab.* 36. the *Rhamnus jujuba*, *Sp. Pl.* 282. *Fl. Zeyl.* N° 89. It bears an eatable fruit, of very little flavor. RHAMNUS JUJUBA.

III.

OTUS BAKKAMOENA.

THE LITTLE HORN OWL.

Strix indica, *Gmelin. Lin.* i. 289. *Latham*, i. 127.
Index Ornith. i. 56. N° 14.

LITTLE HORN OWL.

THIS elegant ſpecies is found in *Ceylon*; is called there *Bakkamoena*, and is a ſcarce ſpecies even in that iſland.

IT is repreſented of its natural ſize. The irides are ſcarlet: the horns take their origin from the baſe of the bill, and point to the ſides of the head: on their inner ſide they are duſky, on their exterior white.

THE bill is duſky, ſurrounded with long briſtles: the circle of feathers round the eyes is of a very pale aſh-color: the external circle of a yellowiſh brown.

THE head of a deep aſh-color: the back duſky: coverts of the wings grey, marked with narrow lines of black, pointing downwards: the quil-feathers regularly barred with black and white: the breaſt buff-colored, marked with ſmall ſagittal black ſpots: the legs feathered half way down: the naked part of a reddiſh yellow.

GLORIOSA SUPERBA.

THE plant is one of the moſt beautiful of the *Indies*;

x but

P. III.

THE LITTLE HORN'D OWL.

but at the ſame time its roots are the moſt venemous. It is found in *Ceylon* and *Malabar*, and, on account of its charming appearance, is called by *Linnæus*, GLORIOSA SUPERBA, *Sp. Pl.* 437. By the natives it is ſtyled *Najajala* and *Nyagbala*, poſſibly from its being poſſeſſed of a poiſon as potent as that of the ſerpent *Naja*, or *Cobra de Capello*, whoſe bite is the moſt fatal of any yet known.

IV.

TROGON FASCIATUS.

THE FASCIATED COUROUCOU*.

Trogon fasciatus, *Gmelin. Lin.* i. 405. *Latham*, ii. 492.
Index Ornith. i. 200.

FASCIATED COUROUCOU.

THIS species is rarely found in the isle of *Ceylon*, where the *Cingalese* call it *Rantvan-kondea.* A species bearing some resemblance to it is described by M. *Brisson*, iv. 165, by the name *Le Couroucou Cendre*; but the bend on the breast, which distinguishes the *Indian* species, evinces it to differ from that of *Cayenne*.

DESCRIPTION.

ITS length was ten inches and an half: the weight one ounce five-eighths.

THE bill black, thick, strong, and arched; the base beset with bristles: the orbits naked, and of a deep blue: the irides yellow.

THE head and neck of a very deep dusky blue, fading into a paler as it approaches the breast.

ACROSS the breast is a fascia or band of white; beneath that the whole under-side is of a bright reddish orange-color.

* Read, on the plate, THE FASCIATED COUROUCOU.

THE

Pl. V.

THE FACEATED COUROUCOU.

The back is tawny; the coverts of the tail grey; the coverts of the wings, and the ſcapulars, elegantly barred with narrow undulated lines of black and white; the quil-feathers duſky, ſtriped with white on their outward webs.

The tail is very long, tipped with black, and compoſed of feathers of unequal lengths; the exterior feathers being much the ſhorteſt.

The legs and feet ſmall and duſky: the toes diſpoſed two backward and two forward, as in the woodpecker tribe.

THE plant is the *Nummularia lactea minima*. *Rumph.* NUMMULARIA.
Amboin. lib. ix. *c.* 78.

V. CUCULUS

V.

CUCULUS PYRRHOCEPHALUS.

THE RED-HEADED CUCKOO.

Cuculus Pyrrhocephalus, *Gmelin. Lin.* i. 417. *Latham*, ii. 544. *Index Ornith.* i. 222.

RED-HEADED CUCKOO.

THE *Cingalese* give this ſpecies the name of *Malkoba:* it inhabits the woods, and lives on fruits.

ITS length is ſixteen inches: its weight four ounces.

THE bill is much arched, ſtrong, and of a greeniſh-yellow color: the crown of the head, and part of the cheeks, are of a bright crimſon, entirely ſurrounded by a band of white. The hind part of the head and neck black, marked with ſmall white ſpots: the fore part of the neck entirely black.

THE back and wings black: the tail very long, compoſed of feathers of unequal lengths; their lower part black, the ends white.

THE breaſt and belly white: the legs of a pale blue.

P. V.

THE RED HEADED CUCKOW.

P VI

THE RED WOODPECKER.

VI.

PICUS MINIATUS.

THE RED WOODPECKER.

Picus Miniatus, *Gmelin. Lin.* i. 432. *Latham,* ii. 595. *Index Ornith.* i. 241.

MR. *Loten* ſhot this on the Highlands of *Java*. It is called by the *Malayans*, *Toekan*, or the Carpenter, a name they give to woodpeckers in general, from the noiſe theſe birds make in boring trees, which reſembles that made by a workman. RED WOODPECKER.

IT is drawn the ſize of life. The bill is of a duſky blue: the head of a deep dull red, and adorned with a long creſt pointing backwards: on the chin is a ſpot of yellow.

THE hind part of the neck, the back, the coverts, and ſecondary feathers of the wings, are of the color of red lead: the fore part of the neck is of a roſe-color: the belly white.

THE quil-feathers black, marked with large white ſpots: the coverts of the tail green: the tail conſiſts of ſharp-pointed feathers, like the *European* kind, and is of a deep blue.

VII. PERDIX

VII.

PERDIX BICALCARATUS.

DOUBLE-SPURRED PARTRIDGE.

Perdix Bicalcarata, *Gmelin. Lin.* ii. 759. *Forster Ind. Zool.* 25.
Ceylon Partridge, *Latham*, iv. 758. *Index Ornith.* ii. 674.

DOUBLE-SPURRED PARTRIDGE.

THE bill of the MALE is red: from that to the region of the eyes is a naked red ſpace. The head is varied with black and white ſtreaks. The whole neck, above and below, is black, elegantly marked with ſagittal lines, the points tending upwards. The thighs white. The primaries duſky, edged with rufous. The back covered with rufous feathers, duſky on each ſide of their ſhafts. Tail duſky. Legs red, on each a pair of ſtrong ſharp ſpurs.

THE head of the female is cinereous. The color of the back and belly rufous, brighteſt below. The tail duſky. Legs red and unarmed.

THESE were taken near *Colombo*. The *Cingaleſe* call them *Haben-Kukella*.

VIII. COLUMBA

VII.

M&F. DOUBLE SPURR'D PARTRIDGE.

LVIII.

THE BLACK CAP'D PIGEON.

VIII.

COLUMBA MELANOCEPHALA.

THE BLACK-CAPPED PIGEON.

Columba Melanocephala, *Gmelin. Lin.* i. 781. *Latham* iv. 654. *Index Ornith.* ii. 610.

THIS most elegant species is painted the size of life. It was found on the ground in the isle of *Java*, having dropped down dead in one of those hot days that are known only in the torrid zone, when the fowls of the air often perish, unable to respire; when lions, leopards, and wolves, immerge themselves up to their nostrils in the water, to preserve themselves from the scorching sun *; and when even men themselves have been forced to ascend the highest trees, in order to draw in a more temperate air †. BLACK-CAPPED PIGEON. HEAT OF THE TORRID ZONE.

SUCH a day occasioned the discovery of this species.

THE fore part of the head, the cheeks, and beginning of the breast, were white: the hind part of the head black: the chin yellow. DESCRIPTION.

* *Boone*'s Account of the Climate and Diseases of *Senegal*.

† *Phil. Transact.* 1767.

The rest of the neck, the breast, upper part of the belly, the back, coverts, and secondary feathers of the wings, of a fine green: the quil-feathers of a dark purple.

The lower belly and vent feathers of a fine yellow: the outside of the thighs green; the inside white: the lower side of the tail crimson: the legs red.

IX. MUSCICAPA

IX.

P. Mazell Sculp.

M&F. FLAMMEOUS. FLYCATCHER.

IX.

MUSCICAPA FLAMMEA.

FLAMMEOUS FLYCATCHER.

Muſcicapa Flammea, *Gmelin. Lin.* ii. 942. *Forſter Ind. Zool.* 25.
Flammeous Flycatcher, *Latham*, iii. 338. *Index Ornith.* ii. 474.

THE bill, head, neck, fore part of the back, and leſſer coverts of the wings, black: reſt of the back bright orange or flame-color: primaries partly black, partly orange: breaſt and belly of the laſt color, ſinking into pale yellow towards the lower belly: tail duſky yellow towards the point: legs black. FLAMMEOUS FLYCATCHER.

THE upper part of the head, and whole back, of the ſuppoſed female, is aſh-colored: about the cheeks and throat duſky: breaſt orange: belly white: acroſs the primaries a flammeous band, bounded above and below with black: tail black above.

THESE are inhabitants of *Ceylon*.

X.

MOTACILLA SUTORIA.

THE TAILOR BIRD.

Motacilla Sutoria, *Gmelin. Lin.* i. 997. *Latham* iv. 515. *Index Ornith.* ii. 551.

TAILOR BIRD.

WONDROUS INSTINCT.

HAD Providence left the feathered tribe unendowed with any particular inſtinct, the birds of the torrid zone would have built their neſts in the ſame unguarded manner as thoſe of *Europe*; but there the leſſer ſpecies, having a certain preſcience of the dangers that ſurround them, and of their own weakneſs, ſuſpend their neſts at the extreme branches of the trees; they are conſcious of inhabiting a climate replete with enemies to them and their young; with ſnakes that twine up the bodies of the trees, and apes that are perpetually in ſearch of prey; but, heaven-inſtructed, they elude the gliding of the one, and the activity of the other.

AN INDIAN FOREST.

AN *Indian* foreſt is a ſcene the moſt pictureſque that can be imagined; the trees ſeem perfectly animated; the fantaſtic monkies give life to the ſtronger branches; and the weaker ſprays wave over your head, charged with vocal and various-plumed inhabitants. It is an error to

P.X

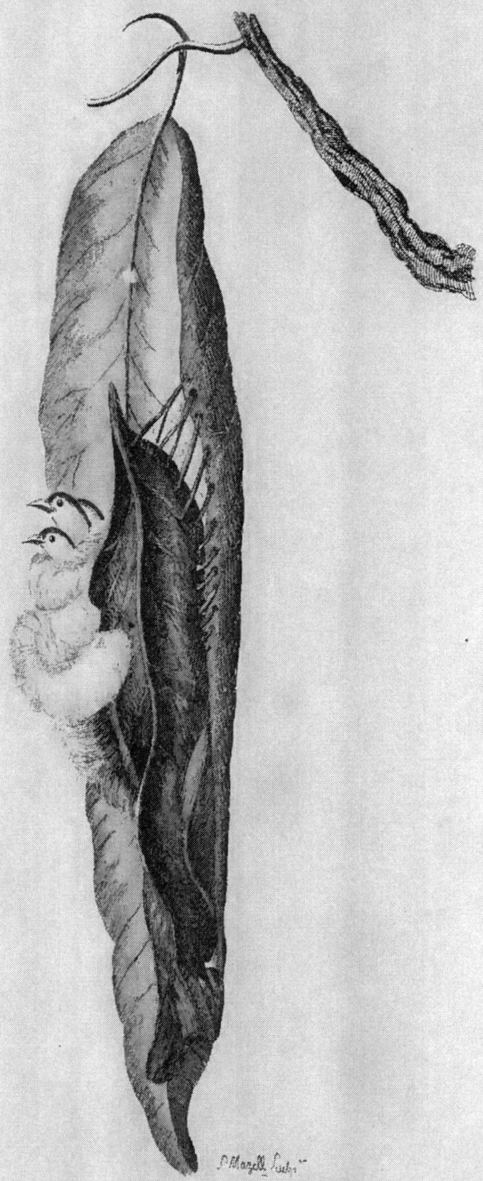

THE TAYLOR BIRD.

ſay that nature hath denied melody to the birds of hot climates, and formed them only to pleaſe the eye with their gaudy plumage: *Ceylon* abounds with birds equal in ſong * to thoſe of *Europe*, which warble among the leaves of trees, groteſque in their appearance, and often loaden with the moſt delicious and ſalubrious fruit. Birds of the richeſt colors croſs the glades, and troops of peacocks complete the charms of the ſcene, ſpreading their plumes to a ſun that has ample powers to do them juſtice. The landſcape, in many parts of *India*, correſponds with the beauties of the animate creation: the mountains are lofty, ſteep, and broken, but cloathed with foreſts, enlivened with cataracts † of a grandeur and figure unknown to this part of the globe.

But to give a reverſe of this enchanting proſpect, which it is impoſſible to enjoy with a ſuitable tranquillity; you are haraſſed in one ſeaſon with a burning heat, or in the other with deluges of rain: you are tormented with clouds of noxious inſects: you dread the ſpring of the *Tiger*, or the mortal bite of the *Naja*.

The brute creation are more at enmity with one another than in other climates; and the birds are obliged to exert unuſual artifice in placing their little broods out of

* That of what the *Portugueſe* call *Dominiquin*, is particularly fine.

† Thoſe of the iſland of *Celebes* are diſtinguiſhed for their magnificent ſcenery, as appears from the drawings in poſſeſſion of Mr. *Loten*.

the

the reach of an invader. Each aims at the ſame end, though by different means. Some form their penſile neſt in ſhape of a purſe, deep, and open at top; others with a hole in the ſide; and others, ſtill more cautious, with an entrance at the very bottom, forming their lodge near the ſummit *.

NEST.

DESCRIPTION.

BUT the little ſpecies we deſcribe, ſeems to have greater diffidence than any of the others: it will not truſt its neſt even to the extremity of a ſlender twig, but makes one more advance to ſafety by fixing it to the leaf itſelf.

IT picks up a dead leaf, and, ſurpriſing to relate, ſews it to the ſide of a living one †, its ſlender bill being its needle, and its thread ſome fine fibres; the lining, feathers goſſamer, and down. Its eggs are white. The color of the bird light-yellow: its length three inches, its weight only three-ſixteenths of an ounce, ſo that the materials of the neſt, and its own ſize, are not likely to draw down a habitation that depends on ſo ſlight a tenure.

* This inſtinct prevales alſo among the birds on the banks of the *Gambia*, in *Africa*, which abounds with monkies and ſnakes: others (for the ſame end) make their neſt in holes of the banks that over-hang that vaſt river. *Purchas*. ii. *p*. 1576.

† The live leaf in the print is that of the *Mango* tree. A neſt of this bird is preſerved in the *Britiſh Muſeum*.

XI. TAN-

XL.

WHITE HEADED IBIS.

XI.

TANTALUS LEUCOCEPHALUS.

THE WHITE-HEADED IBIS.

Tantalus Leucocephalus, *Gmelin. Lin.* i. 649. *Latham*, v. 116. *Index Ornith.* ii. 706.

IN ſize it is much ſuperior to our largeſt curlews. The bill is yellow, very long, and thick at the baſe, and a little incurvated: the noſtrils very narrow, and placed near the head: all the fore part of the head is covered with a bare yellow, and ſeems a continuance of the bill; and the eyes are, in a very ſingular manner, placed very near its baſe.

WHITE-HEADED IBIS.

DESCRIPTION.

THE reſt of the head, the neck, back, belly, and ſecondary feathers, are of a pure white; a tranſverſe broad band of black croſſes the breaſt: the quil-feathers, and coverts of the wings, are black: the coverts of the tail are very long, and of a fine pink color; they hang over and conceal the tail.

THE legs and thighs are very long, and of a dull fleſh-color; the feet ſemi-palmated, or connected by webs as far as the firſt joint.

PLACE. THIS bird was taken in the isle of *Ceylon*, and kept tame for some time at *Colombo*; it made a snapping noise with its bill like a stork; and, what was remarkable, its fine rosy feathers lost their color during the rainy season.

XII. GALLINULA

XII

RED TAIL'D WATERHEN.

XII.

GALLINULA PHŒNICURUS.

THE RED-TAILED WATER-HEN.

Rallus Phœnicurus, *Gmelin. Lin.* i. 715. *Latham*, v. 259. *Index Ornith.* ii. 770.

THIS ſpecies is very common in *Ceylon*, where it is called *Kaloe-kerewaka*, and ſeems the ſame kind that is ſo often figured on the *Indian* papers. RED-TAILED WATER-HEN.

ITS length is nine inches; its weight ſeven ounces and a quarter. DESCRIPTION.

IT has the form of the *European* kind: the bill a little thicker, of a greeniſh caſt, tinged with red; on the fore-head is a fleſh-colored ſpot.

THE hind part of the head and neck, the back and coverts of the wings, are black: the quil-feathers black, marked with large ſpots of a bluiſh caſt.

THE crown of the head, the cheeks, and whole under-ſide of the body, as far as the vent, are of a pure white: the vent feathers, and the tail, of a ferruginous red.

THE legs and feet long, and of a dirty green, tinged with red.

XIII.

ANSER MELANOTOS.

THE BLACK-BACKED GOOSE.

Anſer Melanotos, *Gmelin. Lin.* i. 503. *Latham*, vi. 449. *Index Ornith.* ii. 839.

BLACK-BACKED GOOSE.

NOTWITHSTANDING the iſles of the *Eaſt-Indies* ſwarm with crocodiles, which are animals of inſatiable voracity, catching at every living creature that frequents their element, yet no country abounds more with aquatic birds; nature hath happily given them a quickneſs of ſight, and an inſtantaneous locomotive power, which enables them to elude the jaws of an enemy, which, it is well known, cannot turn without the utmoſt difficulty. It is by a fine inſtinct that the leſſer and more agile ſpecies of ducks frequent, in flocks innumerable, the ſhores, the mouths of rivers, and the marſhy parts of the iſles, and are, with the crocodiles, joint tenants of the waters; while the larger and more clumſy fowl avoid thoſe places, and, dividing into ſmall families, haunt only the lakes and ſtreams that lie * in the deep receſſes of the

* Which *Knox*, in his Hiſtory of *Ceylon*, p. 3, ſays, the crocodiles never approach.

XIII.

BLACK BACK'D GOOSE.

lofty and craggy mountains, protected by the cataracts that prevent the approach of their enemy.

Tame ducks abound so greatly in the isles, that the capture of the wild sort is much neglected. Decoys are unknown there: the commonest method of taking them is this: A man goes into the water with a pot or a hollow calabash on his head, and walks or swims so low as to conceal his whole body: the birds, imagining the gourds to be brought down accidentally, suffer the fowler to approach them; he pulls them by the legs under water, fastens them to a girdle he wears for that purpose, and then proceeds in his sport. This method is also practised in *China* *, and was doubtless introduced there, and into *India*, from *Ægypt*, the original seat of science. INDIAN FOWLING.

The species of goose we now describe, is extremely common in *Ceylon*, and is equal in size to our wild goose: the bill is long, and black; at the base is a knob, which in old birds is very large. DESCRIPTION.

The head and neck are white, marked with small black spots: the breast and belly of a pure white: the back and wings are black, but the ends of the primary feathers of a fine variable green.

The tail is sharp-pointed and black: the legs of the same colour.

* *Du Halde Hist. China*, i. 314.

XIV.

ANAS POIKILORHYNCHUS.

SPOTTED-BILLED DUCK.

Anas Poikilorhyncha, *Gmelin. Lin.* i. 535. *Forster, Ind. Zool.* 23.
Spotted-billed Duck, *Latham*, vi. 487. *Index Ornith.* ii. 850.

SPOTTED-BILLED DUCK.

DESCRIPTION.

THE bill of this species is black, tipt with yellow, and marked on each side of the base with a red spot: a white line passes from thence to and beyond the eye. The cheeks, and under side of the neck and body, white, more and more clouded from the chin to the vent, which is totally black: the wings, back, and tail, are black; each feather slightly edged with white; some of the tertials wholly white: the *speculum* of a variable green, bounded above and below with a narrow line of white.

THIS is the common wild duck of *Ceylon*; and, if I recollect right, is not inferior in size to the *English* wild duck.

XV. ANHINGA

XIV.

SPOTTED BILL DUCK.

XV.

BLACK BELLIED ANHINGA.

XV.

ANHINGA MELANOGASTER.

THE BLACK-BELLIED ANHINGA.

Plotus Melanogaster, *Gmelin. Lin.* i. 580. *Latham*, vi. 624. *Index Ornith.* ii. 895.

WE give it this epithet, to distinguish it from an *American* species with a silvery belly *. BLACK-BELLIED ANHINGA.

THIS kind is found in *Ceylon* and *Java*, but is not peculiar to those islands; a variety, if not the same, being met with in *Senegal* †.

IT sits on the shrubs that hang over the water; and, in a country where every one's ideas are filled with serpents, often terrifies the passengers by shooting out its long slender neck, which, in their first surprize, they take for the darting of some fatal reptile.

ITS body is about the size of that of a common duck, but the neck extremely long: the bill strait, long, and sharp-pointed; the upper part of a pale blue, the lower reddish. DESCRIPTION.

THE eye is very piercing.

* Found in *Brasil.* Vide *Marcgrave, Hist. Brasiliæ*, 218.

† *Planches Enluminées*, 107.

THE

The head and neck and upper part of the breaſt are of a light-brown; each ſide of the head, and the upper part of the neck, marked with a broad white line.

The crop is very large.

The back, ſcapulars, and coverts of the wings, are marked lengthways, in equal portions, with ſtripes of black and white.

The quil-feathers, belly, thighs, and tail, of a deep black; the tail remarkably long and ſlender.

The legs and feet of a pale green; the four toes united by webs, after the manner of thoſe of the corvorant.

XVI.

TIGER SHARK

ZEYLON WRASSE

XVI.

SQUALUS TIGRINUS.

THE TIGER SHARK.

Squalus Tigrinus, *Gmelin. Lin.* i. 1493. *Blcbe*, i. 19. N°4. *Gronov. Muſ.* i. N°136. *Seb. Muſ.* iii. 105. tab. 34. fig. i. *Herman*, tab. Affin. p. 302. *Forſter, Ind. Zool.* 24.

THE head of this ſhark ends obtuſely, being of an equal thickneſs: the noſtrils are at the end of the noſe: at each corner of the mouth is a ſtrong beard: the fins of the back are rounded and contiguous: it is of the diviſion that has the anal fin. The ground-color is duſky: the body marked with white bands paſſing from the back towards the belly: the fins are ſpotted with the ſame color. TIGER SHARK. DESCRIPTION.

THIS ſpecies grows to the length of fifteen feet, and is ſaid to feed on the teſtaceous and cruſtaceous animals of the ſea.

XVII. LABRUS

XVII.

LABRUS ZEYLANICUS.

THE CEYLON WRASSE.

Labrus Zeylanicus, *Gmelin. Lin.* i. 1287. *Forſter, Ind. Zool.* 24.
Labrus Polyodon, *Seb. Muſ.* iii. p. 96. tab. xxxi. fig. 7.

CEYLON WRASSE.

DESCRIPTION.

THIS ſpecies reſembles in form the elegant *European* ſpecies, the *L. Pavo,* and *L. Iulis.* The head is blue: the coverts of the gills green, marked with purple lines: the whole body of a rich green: the dorſal and anal fins purple, edged with pale ſky-blue: on the middle of the pectoral fin is an oblong purple ſpot, environed with light blue: the tail is lunated, the baſe blue: the two ſide rays (which appeared by the drawing to be ſtrong) purple; the intervening rays yellow. The ſize, about a foot and a half.

INHABITS the ſeas of *Ceylon* and *Java:* is called by the *Cingaleſe, Dſchirau-Malu:* by the *Dutch, Papegaay Viſch,* or *Parrot-fiſh*; and is eaten by the common people.

THE

INDIAN FAUNULA.

1

CLASS I. QUADRUPEDS.

DIV. I. HOOFED.

SECT. I. WHOLE-HOOFED.

GENUS.

I.

HORSE.

1. GENEROUS. - HIST. QUAD. vol. i. N° 1.
2. Dshikketi. - - - - - - - - - - — 2.
3. Ass, wild and tame. - - - - - - - - - — 3.

SECT. II. CLOVEN-HOOFED.

II.

Ox.

1. Great Indian. - - - - - - - - - - - - — 6. A.
2. Little. - - - - - - - - - - - - - - — 6. B.
3. Buffalo. - - - - - - - - - - - - - - — 8.
4. Dwarf. - - - - - - - - - - — 8. A.
5. Anoa. - - - - - - - - - - - — 8. B.
6. Guavera. - - - - - - - - - - — 8. C.

III.

SHEEP.

1. Common. - - - - - - - - - - - - - — 11.
2. Wild. - - - - - - - - - - — H. p. 38.
3. Carnero. - - - - - - - - - - — F. p. 35.

IV. GOAT.	1. Domeſtic.	N° 13. a. p. 53.
	2. Caucaſan ?	— 14.
V. ANTELOPE.	1. Algazel.	— 21.
	2. Indian.	— 22.
	3. Indoſtan.	— 26.
	4. White-footed.	— 27.
	5. Common.	— 31.
	6. Smooth-horned.	— β. p. 80.
	7. Chineſe ?	— 36.
VI. DEER.	1. Spotted Axis.	— 47.
	2. Middle-ſized A.	— 48.
	3. Great A.	— 48. *
	4. Porcine.	— 49.
	5. Rib-faced.	— 50.
VII. MUSK.	1. Indian.	— 56.
	2. Guinea.	— 57.
VIII. CAMEL.	1. One-bunched.	— 58.
IX. HOG.	1. Common.	— 61.
	2. Baby-rouſſa.	— 65.
X. RHINOCEROS.	1. One-horned.	— 67.
XI. ELEPHANT.	1. Great.	— 70.

DIV. II.

DIV. II. DIGITATED QUADRUPEDS.

SECT. I. ANTHROPOMORPHOUS.

* TAIL-LESS.

XII. APE.

1. Orang-outang. - - - - - - - - - - - - N° 72.
2. Satyr. - - - - - *Schreber*, 64. tab. ii. B.
3. Long-armed. - - - - - - - - - - - - — 74.
4. Leffer L. armed. - - - - - - - - - - — 74. a.
5. Shaggy. - - - - - - - - - *Lev. Muf.*
6. Golok. - - - - - - *Phil. Tr.* lix. 72.
7. Pygmy. - - - - - - - - - - - - - — 73.
8. Barbary? - - - - - - - *Erxleben*, 14.

** WITH SHORT TAILS. BABOONS.

9. Little. - - - - - - - - - - - - - - — 83.
10. Pig-tail. - - - - - - - - - - - - - — 85.
11. Lion-tailed. - - - - - - - - - - - - — 88.

*** WITH LONG TAILS. MONKIES.

12. Purple-faced. - - - - - - - - - - - — 89.
13. Talapoin. - - - - - - - - - - - - - — 99.
14. Egret. - - - - - - - - - - - - - - — 101.
15. Monea. - - - - - - - - - - - - - - — 102.
16. Chinefe. - - - - - - - - - - - - - — 104.
17. Cochin-china? - - - - - - - - - - - — 107.
18. Tawny. - - - - - - - - - - - - - - — 108.
19. Philippine. - - - - - - - - - - - - — 115.

XIII.
MAUCAUCO. 1. Tail-less. - - - - - - - - - - - - - N° 128.
2. Loris. - - - - - - - - - - - - - - — 129.
3. Tarsier. - - - - - - - - - - - - - - — 133.
4. Flying. - - - - - - - - - - - - - — 135.

SECT. II. RAPACIOUS. CANINE TEETH.

XIV.
DOG. 1. Faithful. - - - - - - - - - - - - - - — 136.
2. Bengal. - - - *De Buffon*, v. tab. xxxiv.
3. Schackal. - - - - - - - - - - - - - - — 145.

XV.
CAT. 1. Lion. - - - - - - - - - - - - - - — 151.
2. Tiger. - - - - - - - - - - - - - - — 152.
3. Panther. - - - - - - - - - - - - - - — 153.
4. Leopard. - - - - - - - - - - - - - —*154.
5. Lesser Leopard. - - - - - - - - - - - — 155.
6. Hunting. - - - - - - - - - - - - - - — 156.
7. Bengal. - - - - - - - - - - - - - - — 164.
8. Lynx. - - - - - - - - - - - - - - — 170. & vol. ii. p. 565.
9. Persian L. - - - - - - - - - - - - - — 173.
10. Serval. - - - - - - - - - - - - - - — 169.

XVI.
BEAR. 1. Brown. - - - - - - - - - - - - - - — 174.

XVII.
BADGER. 1. Indian. - - - - - - - - - - - - - - — 180.

XVIII.
OPOSSUM. 1. Molucca. - - - - - - - - - - - - - — 182.
2. Javan. - - - - - - - - - - - - - - — 183.
3. Phalanger. - - - - - - - - - - - - - — 190.

XIX. WEESEL.	1. Ichneumon. - - - - - - - - - - -		N° 211.
	2. Civet. - - - - - - - - - - - - -		— 223.
	3. Zibet. - - - - - - - - - - - - -		— p. 348.
	4. Fossane. - - - - - - - - - - - - -		— 225.
	5. Zeylan. - - - -	*Gmelin. Lin. Syst.* 89.	
	6. Malacca. - - -	*Sonnerat Voy.* ii. 144.	
	7. Fasciated. - - - - -	*The same*, ii. 193.	

SECT. III. WITHOUT CANINE TEETH, GENERALLY HERBIVOROUS.

XX. CAVIA.	1. Surinam. - - -	HIST. QUAD. vol. ii.	— 238.
XXI. HARE.	1. Common. - - - - - - - - - - - - -		— 241.
	2. Rabbet. - - - - - - - - - - - - -		— 244.
	3. Ogotona. - - - - - - - - - - - - -		— 249.
XXII. PORCUPINE.	1. Crested. - - - - - - - - - - - - -		— 253.
	2. Long-tailed. - - - - - - - - - - -		— 254.
XXIII. SQUIRREL.	1. White-legged. - - - - - - - - - - -		— 266. γ.
	2. Ceylon. - - - - - -	*Ind. Zool.* tab. 1.	— 267.
	3. Javan. - - - - - - - - - - - - - -		— 269.
	4. Bombay - - - - - - - - - - - - - -		— 270.
	5. Ruddy. - - - - - - - - - - - - - -		— 271.
	6. Fair. - - - - - - - - - - - - - - -		— 276.
	7. Palm. - - - - - - - - - - - - - - -		— 279.
	8. Plantane. - - - - - - - - - - - - -		— 280. γ.
	9. Great. - - - - -	*Gmelin. Lin. Syst.* 149.	— 281.
	Dschinschi. - - -	*Gmelin. Lin. Syst.* 151.	

FLYING.

FLYING.

	10. Salient. - - - - - - - - - - - - -	N° 281.
	11. Arrow. - - - *Gmelin. Lin. Syst.* 154.	
XXIV. JERBOA.	1. Middle. - - - - - - - - - - - - - -	— 292. β.
	2. Torrid. - - - - - - - - - - - - - -	— 294.
XXV. RAT.	1. Brown. - - - - - - - - - - - - - -	— 298.
	2. Mouse. - - - - - - - - - - - - - -	— 301.
	3. Oriental. - - - - - - - - - - - - -	— 304.
XXVI. SHREW.	1. Perfuming. - - - - - - - - - - - -	— 337.
	2. Murine. - - - - - - - - - - - - - -	— 340.
XXVII. HEDGE-HOG.	1. Tendrac. - - - - - - - - - - - - -	— 357.

SECT. IV. WITHOUT CUTTING TEETH.

XXVIII. SLOTH.	1. Ursi-form. - - - - - - - - - - - -	
	2. Two-toed. - - - - - - - - - - - - -	— 360.

SECT. V. WITHOUT TEETH.

XXIX. MANIS.	1. Short-tailed. - - - - - - - - - - -	— 368.

XXX. ANT-EATER.

XXX. ANT-EATER.	1. Obfcure. - - - - - - Laft paragraph.	N° 372.
	2. Talgoi. - - - - - - - - - - - - - -	— p. 50.

DIV. III. PINNATED QUADRUPEDS.

XXXI. WALRUS.	1. Indian. - - - - - - - - - - - - - -	— 374.
XXXII. MANATI.	1. Whale-tailed. - - - - - - - - - - - -	— 390.

DIV. IV. WINGED QUADRUPEDS.

XXXIII. BAT.	1. Ternate. - - - - - - - - - - - - -	— 393.
	2. Cordated. - - - - - - - - - - - - -	— 397.
	3. Striped. - - - - - - - - - - - - -	— 404.
	4. Molucca. - - - - - - - - - - - - -	— 405.

CLASS II. BIRDS.

DIV. I. LAND BIRDS.

ORDER I. RAPACIOUS.

THIS Catalogue is taken from MR. LATHAM'S SYNOPSIS OF BIRDS, in Seven Volumes, Quarto (including the Supplement); and from his INDEX ORNITHOLOGICUS, the most complete Work in its kind which I am acquainted with.

GENUS.			LATH. SYN.
I. VULTURE.	1. BENGAL.		I. 19. *pl.* 1.
	2. Pondicherri.	*Son. Voy. Ind.* ii. *p.* 182. *pl.* 104.	VII. 6.
	3. Indian.	*Son. Voy. Ind.* ii. 183. *pl.* 105.	— 6.
	4. Gingi.	*Son. Voy. Ind.* ii. 184.	— 7.
	5. Cheriway.	*Jacquin. Vog. pl.* 4.	— 5.
	6. Secretary.	*Phil. Trans.* lxi. *p.* 55. *tab.* 2.	I. 20. *pl.* 2.
II. FALCON.	1. Cheela.		VII. 33.
	2. Kite.	*Br. Zool.*	I. 61.
	3. Indian.		— 34.* d.
	4. Pondicherri.	*Pl. Enlum.* 416.	— 41.
	5. Javan.	*Index Orn. p.* 27.	
	6. Maritime.	*Licht. Mag.* iv. 2, 6. 20.	
	7. Red Indian.	*Will. p.* 81. *t.* 9.	I. 69.

8. Crested

Genus	Species	Reference	Lath. Syn.
	8. Crested Indian.		I. 80.
	9. White-crested.		— 82.
	10. Pied.	*Ind. Zool.*	I. 81. & VII. 20.
	11. Behree.		VII. 35.
	12. Brown.	*Brown Ill. Zool.* 6. *t.* 3.	I. 96.
	13. Criard.		VII. 38.
	14. Bengal.	*Edw. Birds,* iii. *pl.* 108.	I. 112.
III. Owl.	* Eared.		
	1. Ceylon.	*Brown Ill. p.* 8. *t.* 4.	I. 120. VII. 41.
	2. Coromandel.		VII. 44.
	3. Bakkamuna.	*Ind. Zool.*	I. 127.
	** Without Ears.		
	4. White.	*Br. Zool.*	— 138.
	5. Javan.	*Licht. Mag.* iv. 2. 10. *Index Orn. p.* 64.	— 64.

ORDER II. Pies.

Genus	Species	Reference	Lath. Syn.
IV. Shrike.	1. Malabar.	*Son. Voy. Ind.* ii. *pl.* 111.	VII. 56. *pl.* 108.
	2. Forked-tail.	*Pl. Enl.* 189.	I. 158.
	3. Luzonian.	*Bris.* ii. *pl.* 18. *f.* 1.	— 172.
	4. Antiguan.	*Son. Voy. pl.* 70.	— 171.
	5. Crested-red.	*Edw. Birds, pl.* 54.	— 170.
	6. Jocose.	*Pl. Enl.* 508.	— 175.
	7. Bengal.	*Edw. Birds, pl.* 190.	— 175.
	8. White.	*Son. Voy. pl.* 72.	— 189.
	9. White-billed.	*Pl. Enl.* 9. *f.* 1.	— 181.
	10. Dominican.	*Son. Voy. pl.* 26.	— 181.
	11. Panayan.	*Ibid. pl.* 70.	— 182.
	12. Boulboul.		VII. 57.
	13. Spotted.	*J. R. Forster.*	
V. Parrot.	1. Gingi.	*Pl. Enl.* 239.	I. 209.

2. Amboina

No.	Name	Reference	LATH. SYN.
2.	Amboina red.	*Pl. Enl.* 240.	I. 210.
3.	Blue-headed.	*Pl. Enl.* 192.	— 211.
4.	Indian.	*Edw. pl.* 292.	— 237.
5.	Ofbeck's.	- - -	— 237.
6.	Red-breafted.	*Edw. pl.* 232.	— 212.
7.	Black-crowned.	*Seba,* i. *pl.* 63. *f.* 4.	— 213.
8.	Papuan.	*Son. Voy. pl.* 111.	— 215.
9.	Bornean.	*Edw. pl.* 173.	— 216.
10.	Molucca Lory.	*Pl. Enl.* 519.	— 274.
11.	Coccineous Lory.	*Pl. Enl.* 143.	— 217.
12.	Black-capped Lory.	*Edw. pl.* 170.	— 273.
13.	Beautiful Lory.	- - -	— 217.
14.	Crimfon Lory.	*Pl. Enl.* 518.	— 273.
15.	Gueby Lory.	*Pl. Enl.* 684.	— 219.
16.	Ceram Lory, and Varieties.	- - -	— 269, 270-1.
17.	Variegated Lory.	- - -	— 220.
18.	Purple-capped Lory.	*Edw.* 171. and *Pl. Enl.* 119.	— 271.
19.	Lory Parakeet.	*Edw.* 174.	— 221.
20.	Bontian.	- - -	— 223.
21.	Crimfon-vented.	- - -	— 229.
22.	Varied-winged.	*Son. Voy. pl.* 43.	— 234.
23.	Lace-winged.	*Pl. Enl.* 287.	— 244.
24.	Alexandrine.	*Edw. pl.* 292.	— 234.
25.	Purple-ringed.	*Albin.* ii. *pl.* 18.	— 236.
26.	Muftachoe.	*Pl. Enl.* 517.	— 238.
27.	Bloffom-headed.	*Pl. Enl.* 144.	— 239.
28.	Rofe-headed.	*Edw. pl.* 233.	— 239.
29.	Red-winged.	*Edw. pl.* 236.	— 246.
30.	White-collared.	*Gen. Birds,* 59.	— 251.
31.	Black Cockatoo.	*Edw. pl.* 316.	— 260.
32.	Red-crefted C.	*Edw. pl.* 160.	— 257.
33.	Red-vented C.	*Brown's Ill. pl.* 5.	— 258.
34.	Great White C.	*Pl. Enl.* 263.	— 256.
35.	Red and White C.	- - -	— 260.
36.	Hawk-headed.	*Edw. pl.* 165.	— 266.

37. Red

				LATH. SYN.	
	37.	Red Molucca Lory. - - -	*Pl. Enl.* 519.	I. 274.	
	38.	Grand Lory. - - - - - -	*Pl. Enl.* 683.	— 275.	
	39.	Cochin China. - - - - - - - - - - -		VII. 65.	
	40.	Green and Red Chinese. -	*Edw. pl.* 231.	I. 278.	
	41.	Great-billed. - - - - - -	*Pl. Enl.* 713.	— 278.	
	42.	Amboina Gramineous. - -	*Pl. Enl.* 862.	— 279.	
	43.	Manilla Green. - -	*Brif.* iv. *pl.* 22. *f.* 2.	— 296.	
	44.	Eastern. - - - - - - - - - - - - - -		VII. 64.	
	45.	Amber. - - - - - - - - - - - - - -		— 65.	
	46.	Golden-winged. - - - - -	*Edw. pl.* 293.	I. 309.	
	47.	Blue-rumped. - - - - - - - - - - -		VII. 66.	
	48.	Red and Green. - - - - -	*Edw. pl.* 6.	I. 311.	
	49.	Sapphire-crowned. - - - -	*Edw. pl.* 293.	— 312.	
	50.	Philippine. - - - - - - -	*Pl. Enl.* 520.	— 311.	
	51.	Black-winged. - - - -	*Brown Ill. pl.* 8.	— 316.	
	52.	Collared. - - - - - - -	*Son. Voy. pl.* 39.	— 317.	
	53.	Luzonian. - - - - - - -	*Son. Voy. pl.* 40.	— 318.	
VI. HORN-BILL.	1.	Rhinoceros. - - - - -	*Edw. pl.* 281. B.	— 342.	VII. 69.
	2.	Helmet. - - - - - -	*Edw. pl.* 281. C.	— 343.	
	3.	Philippine.	*Pet. Gaz.* 28. *f.* 6. and *t.* 31. *f.* 1.	— 345.	
	4.	Pied. - - - -	*Son. Voy. Ind.* ii. *pl.* 121.	— 349.	VII. 69.
	5.	Indian. - - - - - - - -	*Pl. Enl.* 283.	— 351.	
	6.	Panayan. - - - - -	*Pl. Enl.* 780, 781.	— 353.	
	7.	Manilla. - - - - - - - -	*Pl. Enl.* 891.	— 354.	
	8.	White. - - - - - - - - - - - - - -		— 357.	
	9.	Wreathed. - - -	*Damp. Voy.* iii, *pl.* 3.	— 358.	VII. 70.
	10.	Gingi. - - -	*Son. Voy. Ind.* ii. *pl.* 121.	VII. 71.	
VII. CROW.	1.	Philippine. - - - - - -	*Pl. Enl.* 603.	I. 381.	
	2.	Short-tailed. - - - - - -	*Pl. Enl.* 258.	— 398.	
	3.	Philippine Sh. tailed. - - -	*Pl. Enl.* 89.	— 398.	A.
	4.	Bengal Sh. tailed. - - -	*Edw. pl.* 324.	— 399.	
	5.	Molucca Sh. tailed. - -	*Pl. Enl. pl.* 257.	— 395.	C.

I

6. Malacca

			Lath. Syn.
	6. Malacca Sh. tailed.	*Son. Voy. Ind.* ii. *pl.* 110.	VII. 81.
	7. Malabar Sh. tailed. - - -	*Id. p.* 191.	— 82. A.
VIII. Roller.	1. Bengal. - - - - - - - -	*Pl. Enl.* 285.	I. 410.
	2. Senegal. - - - - - - - -	*Edw. pl.* 327.	— 408.
	3. Oriental. - - - - - - - -	*Pl. Enl.* 619.	— 411.
	4. Indian. - - - - - - - -	*Edw. pl.* 326.	— 412.
	5. Fairy. - - - - - - - - - - - - -		VII. 87.
	6. Grey-tailed. - - - - - - - - - - - -		— 86.
IX. Oriole.	1. Golden. - - - - - - - - -	*Br. Zool.*	II. 449.
	2. Black-headed. - - -	*Edw. pl.* 77.	— 451.
	3. Yellow. - - - - - - - -	*Edw. pl.* 186.	— 451. B.
	4. Indian. - -	*Aldrov. Av.* i. *pl. in p.* 862.	— 452. D.
X. Grakle.	1. Minor Grakle. - - - - -	*Edw. pl.* 17.	— 455. VII. 90.
	2. Greater Minor. - - - - - -	*Id. ibid.*	— 457.
	3. Bald. - - - - - - - - -	*Pl. Enl.* 200.	— 457.
	4. Paradise. - - - - - - - -	*Pl. Enl.* 219.	— 458.
	5. Dial. - - - - - - - - -	*Edw. pl.* 181.	— 465.
XI. Paradise.	1. Great. - - - - - - - -	*Edw. pl.* 110.	— 471.
	2. King. - - - - - - - - -	*Edw. pl.* 496.	— 475.
	3. Magnificent. - - - - - - -	*Pl. Enl.* 631.	— 477.
	4. Crested. *Wil. Orn.* 92. *Index Orn. p.* 195.		
	5. Gorget. - - - - - - - - - - - - -		II. 478. *pl.* 20.
	6. White-winged - - - - - - - - - - -		VII. 92.
	7. Superb. - - - - - - -	*Pl. Enl.* 632.	II. 479.
	8. Gold-breasted. - - - - -	*Pl. Enl.* 633.	— 481.
	9. Golden. - - - - - - - -	*Edw. pl.* 112.	— 483.
	10. Blue-green. - - - - - -	*Pl. Enl.* 634.	— 482.

11. White.

Genus		Species	Reference	Lath. Syn.
	11.	White. - - - -	*Index Orn. p.* 197. 12.	
	12.	Setaceous.	*Gerin. Orn. t.* 65. *f.* 1.? 197. 12. β.	
XII. Carucui.	1.	Fasciated. - - - - - - - - -	*Ind. Zool.*	II. 492. 7. & β.
	2.	Spotted. - - - - -	*Brown. Ill. pl.* 13.	— 491.
	3.	Blue-cheeked. - - - - - - - - - - -		VII. 93.
	4.	Indian. - - - - - - - - - - - - - -		— 94.
XIII. Barbet.	1.	Philippine. - - - - - -	*Pl. Enl.* 331.	II. 500.
	2.	Black-throated. - - - -	*Son. Voy. pl.* 34.	— 511.
	3.	Great. - - - - - - - -	*Pl. Enl.* 871.?	VII. 95.
	4.	Green. - - - - - - - -	*Pl. Enl.* 870.	II. 504.
	5.	Red-crowned. - - - -	*Brown. Ill. pl.* 14.	— 505.
	6.	Indian. - - - - - - - - - - - - - -		VII. 97.
	7.	Zeylan. - - - - - - -	*Brown. Ill. pl.* 15.	II. 506. VII. 95.
	8.	Gerini? -	*Ger. Orn.* ii. *pl.* 181. *Index Orn. p.* 207.	
XIV. Cuckoo.	1.	Indian spotted. - - - - -	*Edw. pl.* 59.	II. 516.
	2.	Chinese spotted. - - - - -	*Pl. Enl.* 764.	— 519.
	3.	Black. - - - - - - - -	*Pl. Enl.* 274.	VII. 99.
	4.	Coromandel crested. - -	*Pl. Enl.* 872.	II. 520.
	5.	Bengal. - - - - - - -	*Brown Ill. pl.* 13.	— 525.
	6.	Sacred. - - - - - - - -	*Pl. Enl.* 294.	— 526.
	7.	Panayan. - - - - - - -	*Son. Voy. pl.* 79.	— 527.
	8.	Grey-headed. - - - - - - - - - - -		VII. 102.
	9.	Sonnerat's. - - - - - - - - - - - -		— 102.
	10.	Yellow-bellied. - - - - -	*Pl. Enl.* 814.	II. 527.
	11.	Paradise. - - - -	*Bris.* iv. *pl.* 14. A. *f.* 1.	— 529.
	12.	Collared. - - - - - - - -	*Pl. Enl.* 274.	— 529.
	13.	Red-headed. - - - - - - - -	*Ind. Zool.*	— 544.
XV. Wryneck.	1.	Wryneck. - - - - - - - - -	*Br. Zool.*	— 548.

XVI. Wood-

				LATH. SYN.
XVI. WOOD-PECKER.	1.	Little ſpotted. - - - - - -	*Br. Zool.*	II. 566. β. γ.
	2.	Cardinal. - - - - - -	*Son. Voy. pl.* 35.	— 576.
	3.	Brown. - - - - - -	*Pl. Enl.* 748. *f.* 2.	— 577.
	4.	Goa. - - - - - - - - -	*Pl. Enl.* 696.	— 582.
	5.	Bengal. - - - - - - - -	*Edw. pl.* 182.	— 580.
	6.	Ceylon. - - -	*Naturforſch.* xiii. *pl.* 1.	— 581. β.
	7.	Philippine. - - - - - -	*Pl. Enl.* 691.	— 581.
	8.	Manilla. - - - - - - -	*Son. Voy. pl.* 36.	— 583.
	9.	Half-billed. - - - - - - - - - - - -		— 586.
	10.	Red-winged. - - - - - - - -	*Ind. Zool.*	— 595.
	11.	Malacca. - - - - - - - - - - - - -		VII. 111.
XVII. KING-FISHER.	1.	Cape. - - - - - - - -	*Pl. Enl.* 590.	II. 610. VII. 114.
	2.	Black and White. - - - - -	*Edw. pl.* 9.	— 612.
	3.	Great Bengal. - - - - -	*Pl. Enl.* 894.	— 616. B.
	4.	Ten-rou joulon. - - - - -	*Pl. Enl.* 757.	— 617.
	5.	White-collared. -	*Briſ.* iv. *pl.* 37. *f.* 2. A.	— 620.
	6.	Green-headed. - - - -	*Pl. Enl.* 783.	— 620.
	7.	Collared. - - - - - -	*Son. Voy. pl.* 33.	— 623. D.
	8.	Black-capped. - - -	*Son. Voy. pl.* 31.	— 625. A.
	9.	Coromandel. -	*Son. Voy. Ind.* ii. *pl.* 118. *Ind. Orn. p.* 252.	
	10.	Red-headed. - - - - -	*Gen. Birds. pl.* 5.	— 629. & A.
	11.	Purple. - - - - -	*Pl. Enl.* 778. *f.* 2.	— 630.
	12.	Bengal. - - - - - - - - -	*Br. Zool.*	— 631.
	13.	Creſted. - - - - - - - -	*Pl. Enl.* 756.	— 632. 632. β.
	14.	Eaſtern. - - - -	*Briſ.* iv. *pl.* 37. *f.* 1. A.	— 633.
	15.	Ternate. - - - - - - - -	*Pl. Enl.* 116.	— 634.

* THREE-TOED.

1.	Tridactylous. -	*Son. Voy. pl.* 32. *Index Orn.* i. 260.	645.

L XVIII. NUT-

Genus	Species	Reference	Lath. Syn.
XVIII. Nut-hatch.	1. Long-bill.		VII. 118.
XIX. Tody.	1. Variegated.		II. 659.
XX. Bee-eater.	1. Indian.	*Edw. pl.* 183.	— 670.
	2. Philippine.	*Brif.* iv. *pl.* 43. *f* 2.	— 672. C.
	3. Philippine.	*Pl. Enl.* 57.	— 674.
	4. Yellow.	*Will. Orn. pl.* 11.	— 676.
	5. Coromandel.	*Son. Voy. Ind.* ii. *pl.* 119.	VII. 120.
	6. Yellow-throated.		II. 678.
	7. Red-headed.	*Brif.* iv. *pl.* 44. *f.* 3. A.	— 679.
	8. Molucca.		— 684.
	Common. *European.*		— 667.
XXI Hoopo.	1. Crefted.	*Br. Zool.*	II. 687. VII. 122.
	2. Crefted Promerops.	*Seb.* i. *t.* 30. *f.* 5.	— 691.
	3. Red-billed Pr.		VII. 124. *pl.* 110.
	4. Blue.		— *ibid.*
XXII. Creeper.	1. Familiar?	*Br. Zool.*	II. 701.
	2. Manilla.		— 706. A.
	3. Red-breafted.	*Pl. Enl.* 246.	— 706. 8.
	4. Brown and White.	*Edw. pl.* 26.	— 707. A.
	5. Luzonian.	*Son. Voy. pl.* 30. D.	— 708. B.
	6. Philippine.	*Pl. Enl.* 576. 1.	— 711.
	7. Collared.	*Edw. pl.* 265.	— 709.
	8. Ceylon.		— 713. A.
	9. Grey.	*Pl. Enl.* 576. *f.* 2.	— 714.
	10. Little.	*Pl. Enl.* 576. *f.* 3.	— 714. A.
	11. Lotenian.	*Pl. Enl.* 575. *f.* 2. 3.	— 715.
	12. Green-gold.	*Seb. Th. pl.* 69. *f.* 5.	— 716.

			Lath. Syn.
13.	Asiatic.	*Index Orn.* i. 288.	
14.	Red-backed.	*Son. Voy. Ind.* ii. *pl.* 117. *f.* 1.	VII. 132.
15.	Red-spotted.	*Edw. pl.* 81.	II. 736.
16.	Indigo.		VII. 130.
17.	Yellow-bellied.	*Son. Voy. Ind.* ii. *pl.* 116. *f.* 1.	— 131.
18.	Tufted.		— 132.
19.	Red-billed.		— 133.
20.	Yellow-winged.		— 133.
21.	Long-billed.		— 133.
22.	Macassar.	*Seb.* i. *pl.* 63. *f.* 1.	II. 741.
23.	Indian.	*Seb.* ii. *pl.* 19. *f.* 2.	— 741.
24.	Amboina.	*Seb.* ii. *pl.* 62. *f.* 2.	— 741.

ORDER. III. Passerine.

XXIII. Stare.

1.	Contra.	*Edw. pl.* 187.	III. 5.

XXIV. Thrush.

1.	Pagoda.		— 30. VII. 140.
2.	Malabar.		— 30. VII. 140.
3.	Chinese.	*Bris.* ii. *pl.* 23. *f.* 1.	— 36.
4.	Philippine.		— 38.
5.	Surat.		— 38.
6.	Pensive.	*Pl. Enl.* 636. 564.	— 53.
7.	Hermit.	*Pl. Enl.* 339.	— 54.
8.	Pigeon.		— 64.
9.	Dominican.	*Pl. Enl.* 627. 2.	— 58.
10.	Songster.	*Son. Voy. pl.* 73.	— 59.
11.	Malabar.		— 60.
12.	Ceylon.	*Edw. pl.* 321.	— 62.
13.	Orange-headed.		VII. 145.
14.	Indian.	*Pl. Enl.* 564. 1.	III. 66.
15.	Grey.		— 67.
16.	Mindanao.	*Pl. Enl.* 627. 1.	— 69.

Genus	Species	Reference	Lath. Syn.
	17. Long-tailed.		III. 72. *pl.* 39.
	18. Amboina.	*Seb.* i. *pl.* 62. *f.* 4.	— 73.
	19. Yellow-crowned.	*Brown Ill. pl.* 22.	— 74. VII. 143.
	20. Ash-rumped.	*Pl. Enl.* 273. 2.	— 74.
	21. Gingi.		VII. 144.
	22. Dauma.		— 145.
	23. Black and Scarlet.		— 146.
	24. Rose-colored.	*Edw. pl.* 20.	— 142.
	Rock. *European.*		III. 57.
XXV. Coly.	1. Panayan.	*Son. Voy. pl.* 74.	— 103.
	2. Indian.		VII. 147.
XXVI. Grosbeak.	1. Gold-backed.	*Brown Ill. pl.* 25.	III. 115.
	2. Cardinal.	*Mus. Carls. fasc* ii. *t.* 41.	— 118. β.
	3. Boeton.	*Seb.* i. *pl.* 60. *f.* 4.	— 119.
	4. Madagascar.	*Pl. Enl.* 134. 2.	— 119.
	5. Java.	*Edw. pl.* 41. 42.	— 129.
	6. Philippine.	*Pl. Enl.* 135. 2.	— 129.
	7. Bengal.	*Edw. pl.* 189.	— 133.
	8. Sumatran.	*Mus. Carls. fasc.* iii. *t.* 71. *Index Orn.* 384.	
	9. Yellow?		— 139.
	10. Yellow-rumped.		— 140.
	11. Malacca.	*Edw. pl.* 355.	— 140.
	12. Molucca.	*Pl. Enl.* 139. 2.	— 141.
	13. Cowry.	*Edw. pl.* 40.	— 142.
	14. Brown?		— 147.
	15. Lineated?	*Bris.* iii. *pl.* 17. 1.	— 149.
	16. Red-billed.	*Edw. pl.* 271. 2.	— 151.
	17. Cinereous.	*Edw. pl.* 179. 2.	— 154.
	18. Indian.		VII. 155.
	19. Malabar.		III. 154.

20. Orange-

			Lath. Syn.
	20. Orange-bellied. - - - -	*Edw. pl.* 83. 1.	III. 157.
	21. Prasine. - -	*Mus. Carls. fasc.* iii. *t.* 73. *Index Orn.* i. 396.	
	22. Dwarf. - - - -	*Jacq. Vog. p.* 28. *pl.* 13.	— 158.
XXVII. Bunting.	1. Long-tailed. - - - - -	*Will. Orn. t.* 45.	— 181.
	2. Panayan. - - - - - - - -	*Pl. Enl.* 647.	— 184.
	3. Familiar. - - - - - - - - - - - - -		— 194.
	4. Red-rumped. - - - -	*Pl. Enl.* 101. 2.	— 208.
	5. Blue-faced. - - - -	*Bris.* iii. *pl.* 7. *f.* 4.	— 209.
	6. Green. - - - - - - - - - - - - - -		— 209.
	7. Asiatic. - - - - - - - - - - - - - -		VII. 160.
XXVIII. Tanagre.	1. Amboina. - - - - -	*Seb.* i. *pl.* 38. *f.* 6.	III. 244.
XXIX. Finch.	1. Lovely. - - - - - - - - - - - - - -		VII. 168.
	2. White-breasted. - - - -	*Pl. Enl.* 224. 2.	III. 268.
	3. Collared. - - - - - - - -	*Edw. pl.* 272.	— 280.
	4. Blue-bellied. - - - - - - -	*Edw. pl.* 131.	— 310.
	5. Amandavad. - - - -	*Edw. pl.* 355. 1.	— 311.
	6. Brown. - - - - - - -	*Pl. Enl.* 115. 2.	— 312.
	7. Maia, or Cuba. - -	*Pl. Enl.* 109. 2. *fem.*	— 315.
	8. Ceylon. - - - - - - - - - - - - - -		— 317.
	9. Lunar. - - - - - - - -	*Mill. Ill. pl.* 30.	— 320.
	10. Green-rumped. - - - - - - - - - - -		— 320.
XXX. Fly-catcher.	1. Pied. - - - - -	*Br. Zool. Edw. pl.* 30.	— 324.
	2. Coromandel. - - - - - - - - - - - -		— 331.
	3. Flammeous. - - - - - - - -	*Ind. Zool.*	— 338.
	4. Cinnamon. - - - - - - - - - - - - - -		IV. 447. 42.
	5. Tufted. - - - - - - - - - - - - - -		III. 334.

6, Red-

			Lath. Syn.
	6. Red-vented. - - - - -	*Brown Ill. pl.* 31.	III. 335.
	7. Variety. Yellow-vented. - - - -		— *ibid.*
	8. Guava. - - - - - -	*Son. Voy. pl.* 28.	— *ibid.*
	9. Yellow-breasted. - -	*Brown Ill. pl.* 82.	— 336.
	10. Green. - - - - - - - - - - - - - -		— 336.
	11. Black. - - - - - -	*Son. Voy. pl.* 27. 2.	— 338.
	12. Philippine. - - - - - - - - - - - -		— 339.
	13. Azure. - - - - - -	*Pl. Enl.* 666. 1.	— 339.
	14. Blue-head. - - - - -	*Son. Voy. pl.* 26. 1.	— 339.
	15. Yellow-throat. - -	*Son. Voy. pl.* 26. 2.	— 340.
	16. Paradise. - - - - - - -	*Edw. pl.* 113.	— 345.
	17. Javan. - -	*Mus. Carls. fasc.* iii. *t.* 75. *Index Orn.* ii. 490.	
	18. Cambaian - - - - - - - - - - - - -		— 490.
XXXI. Lark.	1. Sky? - - - - - - - - - -	*Br. Zool.*	IV. 368.
	2. Malabar. - -	*Son. Voy. Ind.* ii. *pl.* 113. 1.	— 379.
	3. Gingi. - -	*Son. Voy. Ind.* ii. *pl.* 113. 2.	— 380.
XXXII. Wagtail.	1. White? - - - - - - - - - -	*Br. Zool.*	— 395.
	2. Collared. - - - - - -	*Son. Voy. pl.* 29.	— 396.
	3. Pied. - - - - - - -	*Raii Syn. pl.* 1. *f.* 1.	— 397.
	4. Javan. - - - - - - - -	*Br. Zool. var.*	— 398. 399.
	5. Indian. - - - - - - - - - - - - - -		— 399.
	6. Yellow. - - - - - -	*Br. Zool.* Timor.	— 401. 6. A.
	7. Green. - - - - - -	*Brown Ill. pl.* 33.	— 403.
XXXIII. Warbler.	1. Luzonian. - - - - -	*Pl. Enl.* 235. 1. 2.	— 451.
	2. Coromandel. - - - - - - - - - - - - -		— 452.
	3. Philippine. - - - - -	*Pl. Enl.* 185. 2.	— 453.
	4. Wheat-ear. - - - - - - - - -	*Br. Zool.*	— 465.
	5. Pink. - - - - - -	*Brown Ill. pl.* 33.	— 473.

6. Olive.

			Lath. Syn.
	6. Olive. - - - - - -	*Brown Ill. pl.* 14.	IV. 473.
	7. Green. - - - - - - - -	*Edw. pl.* 79.	— 474.
	8. Cingalese. - - - - -	*Brown Ill. pl.* 32.	— 474.
	9. Superb. - - - - - - - - - - - - -		— 501. *pl.* 53.
	10. Blue headed. -	*Son. Voy. t.* 27. 1. *Index Orn.* ii. 545.	
	11. Gold-crested Wren. - - - - -	*Br. Zool.*	III. 508.
	12. Tailor. - - - - - - - - -	*Ind. Zool.*	— 515.
	13. Black-necked. - - - - - - - - - - -		VII. 187.
	14. Cambaian. - - - - -	*Index Orn.* ii. 554.	
	15. Guzurat. - - - - - - - - - -	*Ibid.*	
	16. Asiatic. - - - - - - - - - - -	*Ibid.*	
	Yellow Wren. - - - - - -	*Br. Zool.*	IV. 512.
XXXIV. Manakin.	1. Little. - - - - - - - - - - - - - -		— 526.
XXXV. Titmouse.	1. Malabar. - - -	*Son. Voy. Ind.* ii. *pl.* 114. 1.	— 555.
	2. Indian. - - -	*Mus. Carls. fasc.* ii. *t.* 50. *Index Orn.* ii. 572.	
XXXVI. Swallow.	1. Panayan. - - - - - -	*Son. Voy. pl.* 76.	— 565.
	2. Red-headed. - - - - - - - - - -		— 571.
	3. Indian. - - - - - - - - - - - - -		— 571. *pl.* 56.
	4. Esculent. - - - -	*Bris.* ii. *pl.* 46. *f.* 2. A.	— 578.
	Chimney. - - - - - - - - -	*Br. Zool.*	— 560.
XXXVII. Goat-sucker.	1. Asiatic. - - - - - - - - - - - - - -		VII. 195.
	2. Indian. - - - - - - - - - - - - - -		— 196.

ORDER IV. Columbine.

* Tail even at the End.

			Lath. Syn.
XXXVIII. Pigeon.	1. Domeſtic. - - - - - - -	*Pl. Enl.* 466.	IV. 605.
	2. Laced. - - - - - - - - - - - - - -		— 610.
	3. White-wniged. - - - - -	*Edw. pl.* 76.	— 617. VII. 197.
	4. Great-crowned. - - - - -	*Edw. pl.* 338.	— 620.
	5. Leſſer-crowned. -	*Son. Voy. Ind.* ii. *pl.* 100.	— 622. 623. *pl.* 58.
	6. Grey-headed. - - - -	*Son. Voy. pl.* 66.	— 623.
	7. Yellow-faced. - - -	*Brown Ill. pl.* 20.	— 624.
	8. Purple ſhoulder. - - - - - - - - - -		VII. 201.
	9. Aſiatic. - - - - - - - - - - - - -		— 202.
	10. Green-winged. - - - - -	*Edw. pl.* 14.	IV. 625.
	11. Jamboo. - - - - - - - - - - - - -		— 627.
	12. Red-crowned. - - - -	*Son. Voy. pl.* 67.	— 628.
	13. Parrot. - *Pl. Enl.* 138.	*Son. Voy. pl.* 65.	— 629. 630.
	14. Aromatic. - - - - - -	*Pl. Enl.* 163.	— 631.
	15. Nicobar. - - - - - - - -	*Pl. Enl.* 491.	— 642.
	16. Common Turtle. - - -	*Pl. Enl.* 394.	— 644.
	17. Luzonian T. - - - - -	*Son. Voy. pl.* 22.	— 646.
	18. Collared. - - - - - - - -	*Pl. Enl.* 244.	— 648.
	19. Grey. - - -	*Son. Voy. Ind.* ii. *pl.* 102.	— 649.
	20. Barred. - - - - - - - - -	*Edw. pl.* 16.	— 650. VII. 200.
	21. Surat. - - - - - -	*Index Orn.* ii. 609.	
	22. Cambayan. - - - - - - - - - - - -		— 652.
	23. Malabar. - - - - - - - - - - - - -		— 652.
	24. Green. - - - - - - - - -	*Pl. Enl.* 142.	— 653.
	25. Black-capped. - - - - - -	*Ind. Zool.*	— 654.
	26. Javan. - - - - - - - - -	*Pl. Enl.* 177.	— 654.
	27. Blue-crowned. - - - - - - - - - - -		— 655.
	28. Red-breaſted. - - - - -	*Son. Voy. pl.* 21.	— 657.
	29. Sanguine. - - - - - -	*Son. Voy. pl.* 20.	— 657.
	30. Malacca. - - - - - - - - - - - - -		— 661.

* * Long

	** LONG AND CUNEIFORM TAILS.		LATH. SYN.
	31. Amboina. - - - - -	*Brif.* i. *pl.* 9. *f.* 3.	IV. 665.
	32. Bantam. - -	*Muf. Carlf. fafc.* iii. *t.* 67. *Index Orn.* ii. 615.	

ORDER V. GALLINACEOUS.

XXXIX. PEACOCK.	1. Crefted. - - - - -	*Pl. Enl.* 433. 434.	IV. 668. *pl.* 60.
XL. TURKY.	1. Horned. - - - - - - - -	*Edw. pl.* 16.	— 680.
XLI. PHEASANT.	1. Wild Cock. -	*Son. Voy. Ind.* ii. *pl.* 94. 95.	— 698.
	2. Colored. - - - - - - - - - - - - - -		VII. 210.
	3. Impèyan. - - - - - - - - - - - - -		— 208. *pl.* 114.
XLII. PARTRIDGE.	1. Ceylon. - - - - - - - - -	*Ind. Zool.*	IV. 758. VII. 222.
	2. Francolin. - - - - - - -	*Edw. pl.* 246.	— 759.
	3. Hackled. - - - - - - - - - - - - -		— 766. *pl.* 66.
	4. Red. - - - - - - - -	*Pl. Enl.* 150. 231.	— 767.
	5. Gingi. - - - - - - - - - - - - - -		— 773.
	6. Pondicherri. - - - - - - - - - - - -		— 774.
	7. Fafciated. - - - - - - - - - - - - -		— 221.
	8. Afiatic. - - - - - - -	*Index Orn.* ii. 649.	
	9. Indian. - - - - - - - - - - - - - -		— 752. 20.
	10. Javan. - - - - - - -	*Brown Ill. pl.* 17.	— 775.
	11. Common Quail. - - - - -	*Pl. Enl.* 170.	— 779.
	12. Chinefe. - - - - - - - -	*Edw. pl.* 247.	— 783.
	13. Noify. - - - - - - -	*Will. Orn. pl.* 29.	— 787.
	14. Coromandel. - - - - - - - - - - - -		— 789.
	15. Manilla. - - - - - - -	*Son. Voy. pl.* 24.	— 790.

			LATH. SYN.
	16. Cambaian. - - - -	*Index Orn.* ii. 655.	

* TRIDACTYLOUS.

	1. Luzonian. - - - - - -	*Son. Voy. pl.* 23.	IV. 792.
XLIII. BUSTARD.	1. Indian. - - - - - - -	*Edw. pl.* 250.	— 804.
	2. Passarage. - - - - - - - - - -		VII. 228.
	3. White-chinned. - - -	*Mill. Ill. pl.* 33.	IV. 806.
XLIV. CASUARY.	1. Galeated. - - - - - -	*Pl. Enl.* 313.	V. 10. *pl.* 72.

DIV. II. WATER FOWL.

ORDER. VII. CLOVEN-FOOTED.

XLV. SPOON-BILL.	1. Luzonian. -	*Son. Voy. pl.* 51. *Index Orn.* ii. 668. β.	
XLVI. JABIRU.	1. Indian. - - - - - - - - - - - - -		VII. 231.

* CRANES.

XLVII. HERON.	1. Sibirian Crane. - - -	*Pallas It.* ii. *t.* 1.	V. 37.
	2. Indian Crane. - - - - - -	*Edw.* 45.	— 38. 39.
	3. Common Crane. - - - -	*Pl. Enl.* 769.	— 40.

			LATH. SYN.
	4. Japan Crane. - - - - - - - - - - - - -		V. 42.
	5. Gigantic. - - - - - - - - - - - - - -		— 45. VII. 232. *pl.* 115.

** HERONS.

	6. Philippine Heron. - - - -	*Pl. Enl.* 898.	— 72.
	7. Coromandel. - - - - -	*Pl. Enl.* 910.	— 75. A.
	8. Cinnamon. - - - - - - - - - - - - -		— 77.
	9. Malacca. - - - - - - - -	*Pl. Enl.* 911.	— 78.
	10. Violet. - - - - - - - -	*Pl. Enl.* 906.	— 97.
	11. Louhaujung. - - - - - - - - - - - -		VII. 238.
	12. Yellow-necked. - - - - - - - - - - -		— 239.

*** BEC-OUVERTS.

	13. Pondicherry. - - - -	*Pl. Enl.* 932.	V. 101.
	14. Coromandel. -	*Son. Voy. Ind.* ii. *pl. p.* 219.	— 102.
XLVIII. IBIS.	1. White-headed. - - - - - -	*Ind. Zool.*	— 116.
	2. Manilla. - - - - - -	*Son. Voy. pl.* 47.	— 117.
	3. Black-headed. - - - - - - - - - - -		VII. 240.
XLIX. CURLEW.	1. Luzonian. - - - - -	*Son. Voy. pl.* 48.	V. 122.
L. SNIPE.	1. Woodcock? - - - - - - -	*Br. Zool.*	— 129.
	2. Common Snipe. - - - - - -	*Br. Zool.*	— 134.
	3. Cape. - - - - - - - - - - - - -		VII. 244. E.
	4. Bengal. - - - - - -	*Albin.* iii. *pl.* 90.	V. 140. D.
	5. Madras. - - - - -	*Raii Syn. t.* 1. *f.* 2.	— 141.

6. White

			LATH. SYN.
	6. White Indian. - - - - - - - - - - - -		V. 141.
LI. SAND-PIPER.	1. Goa. - - - - - - - - -	*Pl. Enl.* 807.	— 165.
LII. PLOVER.	1. Golden? - - - - - - - - -	*Br. Zool.*	— 193.
	2. Long-legged. - - - - - - - -	*Br. Zool.*	— 195. VII. 252.
	3. Philippine. - - - - -	*Son. Voy. pl.* 46.	— 205. C.
	4. Wattled. - - - - - - -	*Pl. Enl.* 880.	— 216.
	5. Indian. - - - - - - - - - - - - - - -		VII. 254.
LIII. RUNNER. CURSORIUS. LATHAM *Index*, ii. 751.	1. Coromandel Pl. - - - - -	*Pl. Enl.* 892.	V. 217.
LIV. PRATINCOLE.	1. Maldivian. - - - - - - - - - - - -		— 224.
	2. Coromandel. - - - - - - - - - - - -		— *ibid.*
	3. Madras. - - - - - - - - - - - - - -		— *ibid.*
LV. RAIL.	1. Philippine. - - - - - - -	*Pl. Enl.* 774.	— 230.
	2. Striated Ph. - - - -	*Brif.* v. *pl.* 14. *f.* 2.	— 232. C.
	3. Dusky. - - - - - - - - - - - - - -		— 232. B.
	4. Banded. - - - - -	*Brif.* v. *pl.* 15. *f.* 1.	— 233.
	5. Brown. - - - - - - - - -	*Pl. Enl.* 773.	— *ibid.*
	6. Ceylon. - - - - - - -	*Brown Ill. pl.* 37.	— 235.
LVI. JACANA.	1. Luzonian. - - - - - - -	*Son. Voy. pl.* 45.	— 245.
	2. Indian. . - - - - - - - - - - - - -		VII. 257.

LVII. GALLINULE.

			Lath. Syn.
LVII. Gallinule.	1. Madras. - - - - -	*Raii Syn. t.* 1. *f.* 4.	V. 253.
	2. Purple. - - - - - - -	*Edw. pl.* 87.	— 254.
	3. Green. - - - - - - - - - - - - - -		— 257.
	4. Red-tailed. - - - - - - -	*Ind. Zool.*	— 259.
	5. Crested. - - - - - - - - - - - - -		— 267.

ORDER VIII. Pinnated Feet.

LVIII. Grebe.	1. Little. - - - - - - -	*Pl. Enl.* 945.	— 290. A.

ORDER IX. Web-Footed.

LIX. Albatros.	1. Wandering. - - - - - -	*Edw. pl.* 88.	— 304.
LX. Skimmer.	1. Black. - - - - - - - -	*Pl. Enl.* 357.	VI. 347.
LXI. Tern.	1. Caspian. - - - -	*Index Orn.* ii. 804. β.	
	2. Philippine. - - - - -	*Son. Voy. pl.* 85.	VII. 267.
	3. Panayan. - - - - - -	*Son. Voy. pl.* 84.	VI. 363.
	4. White. - - -	*Portlock Voy. pl. p.* 312.	— 363. VII. 266.
LXII. Petrel.	1. Stormy. - - - - - - - -	*Edw. pl.* 90.	— 411.
LXIII. Duck.	1. Chinese? - - - - - - -	*Pl. Enl.* 374.	— 447.
	2. Black-backed. - - - - - -	*Ind. Zool.*	— 449.

3. Barred.

			LATH. SYN.
	3. Barred-head. - - - - - - - - - - - -		VII. 177.
	4. Greyhead. - - - -	*Brown Ill. pl.* 41. 42.	VI. 458.
	5. Spotted-bill. - - - - - - - -	*Ind. Zool.*	— 487.
	6. Falcated. - - - - - - -	*Pl. Enl.* 930.	— 517. A.
	7. Pink-headed. - - - - - - - - - - - -		VII. 276. *pl.* 119.
	8. Coromandel. - - - -	*Pl. Enl.* 949. 950.	VI. 556.
	9. Manilla. - - - - - - -	*Son. Voy. t.* 54.	— 557.
LXIV. PELECAN.	1. White. - - - - - - - -	*Edw. pl.* 92.	— 575.
	2. Roseate. - - - - - -	*Son. Voy. pl.* 54.	— 579.
	3. Manilla. - - - - - -	*Son. Voy. pl.* 53.	— 583.
	4. Philippine. - - - - -	*Brif.* vi. *pl.* 46.	— 583.
LXV. DARTER.	1. Black-bellied. - - - - - -	*Ind. Zool.*	— 624.

CLASS

CLASS III. AMPHIBIA.

ORDO I. REPTILIA.

Genus.		
I. Testudo.	Imbricata. - - - - - -	*Seb. Muf.* i. *tab.* 80. *fig.* 9.
	Squamata. - - - - - - - - - - - - -	*Bont. Java.* 82.
	Lutaria. - - - - - - - - - -	*Amœn. Acad.* i. *p.* 139. N° 23.
	Serpentina. - - - - - - - - - - -	*Muf. Ad. Fr.* 2. *p.* 36.
	Indica. - - - - - - - - - -	-*Schneid. Schild. p.* 355. N° 14.
II. Rana.	Gibbofa. - - - - - - - - - -	*Seb. Muf.* i. *tab.* 71. *fig.* 4. 5.
	Ventricofa. - - - - - - - - - -	*Seb. Muf.* i. *tab.* 74. *fig.* 1.
	Venulofa. - - - - - - - - - - -	*Seb. Muf.* i. *tab.* 72. *fig.* 4.
	Marginata. - - - - - - - - - - - -	*Muf. Ad. Fr.* i. *p.* 47.
III. Draco.	Volans. - - - - - - - - - - - -	*Seb. Muf.* ii. *tab.* 86. *fig.* 3.
IV. Lacerta.	Gangetica. - - - - - - - -	*Edw. Act. Ang.* 49. *p.* 639. *t.* 19.
	Monitor. - - - - - - - - - -	*Seb. Muf.* ii. *tab.* 86. *fig.* 2. 2.
	Bicarinata.	
	Mauritanica. - - - - - -	β. *Seb. Muf* i. *tab.* 108. *fig.* 2. 7.
	Iguana. - - - - - - - - - -	*Seb. Muf.* i. *tab.* 95. *fig.* 1. 2.
	Calotes. - - - - - - - - - - -	*Seb. Muf.* i. *tab.* 86. *fig.* 6.

Superciliofa.

Superciliosa. - - - - - - - - - - *Seb. Mus.* i. *tab.* 94. *fig.* 4.
Scutata. - - - - - - - - - - *Seb. Mus.* i. *tab.* 109. *fig.* 3. 4.
Amboinensis, & Var. β.
Lacustris. - - - - - - - - - - γ. *Seb. Mus.* ii. *tab.* 12. *fig.* 7.
Vittata. - - - - - - - - - - - *Houtt. Act. Ulissing.* 9. *t.* 2.
Gecho. - - - - - - - - - - - *Forsk. Fn. Arab. p.* 13. N° 4.
Chamæleon. - - - - - - - - *Seb. Mus.* i. *tab.* 82. *fig.* 2. 4. 5.
Agilis. - - - - - - - - - - - *Seb. Mus.* ii. *tab.* 79. *fig.* 5.
Tequixin. - - - - - - - - - - *Seb. Mus.* i. *tab.* 96. *fig.* 1.
Plica.
Serpens.
Bipes. - - - - - - - - - - - - *Seb. Mus.* i. *tab.* 53. *fig.* 8.

ORDO II. SERPENTES.

V.
BOA. Hipnale. - - - - - - - - - - *Seb. Mus.* ii. *tab.* 34. *fig.* 2.
Constrictor. - - - - - - - - - - *Seb. Mus.* i. *tab.* 36. *fig.* 5.

VI.
COLUBER. Clotho. - - - - - - - - - - - *Seb. Mus.* ii. *tab.* 93.
Lutrix.
Plicatilis. - - - - - - - - - - - *Seb. Mus.* ii. *tab.* 57. *fig.* 5.
Alidras.
Buccatus. - - - - - - - - - - *Mus. Ad. Fr.* i. *tab.* 19. *fig.* 3.
Javanus. - - - - - - - - - - - *Seb. Mus.* i. *tab.* 10. *fig.* 2.
Berus. - - - - - - - - - - β. δ. *Seb. Mus.* ii. *tab.* 9. *fig.* 8.
Typhlus.
Reginæ. - - - - - - - - - - *Mus. Ad. Fr.* i. *tab.* 13. *fig.* 3.
Æsculapii. - - - - - - - - - *Mus. Ad. Fr.* i. *tab.* 11. *fig.* 2.
Rhombeatus. - - - - - - - - *Mus. Ad. Fr.* i. *tab.* 24. *fig.* 2.
Miliaris. - - - - - - - - - - - - *Mus. Ad. Fr.* i. *p.* 27.
Albus. - - - - - - - - - *Mus. Ad. Fr.* i. *p.* 24. *t.* 14. *fig.* 2.
Agilis. - - - - - - - - - - *Mus. Ad. Fr.* i. *tab.* 21. *fig.* 2.

	Lacteus.	*Muf. Ad. Fr.* i. *tab.* 18. *fig.* 1.
	Pallidus.	*Ibid. tab.* 7. *fig.* 2.
	Cæcus.	*Seb. Muf.* ii. *tab.* 90. *fig.* 1.
	Naja.	*Seb. Muf.* i. *tab.* 44. *fig.* 1.
	Padera.	*Muf. Ad. Fr.* ii. *p.* 44.
	Canus.	*Muf. Ad. Fr.* i. *p.* 31. *t.* 11. *fig.* 1.
	Zeylonicus.	*Seb. Muf.* i. *tab.* 100. *fig.* 4.
	Laticaudatus.	*Muf. Ad. Fr.* i. *tab.* 16. *fig.* 1.
	Atrox.	β. *Seb. Muf.* i. *tab.* 43. *fig.* 4. 5.
	Saturninus.	*Muf. Ad. Fr.* i. *tab.* 9. *fig.* 1.
	Candidus.	*Ibid. tab.* 7. *fig.* 1.
	Scaber.	*Ibid. tab.* 10. *fig.* 1.
	Carinatus.	
	Exoletus.	*Ibid. tab.* 10. *fig.* 2.
	Trifcalis.	
	Pelias.	
	Ocellatus.	*Seb. Muf* ii. *tab.* 1. *fig.* 3. 8.
	Hitambocia.	*Seb. Muf.* i. *tab.* 33. *fig.* 6.
	Tigrinus.	*Seb. Muf.* ii. *tab.* 15. *fig.* 2.
	Molurus.	
	Ahætulla.	*Catefb. Car.* ii. *tab.* 47.
	Petalarius.	*Muf. Ad. Fr.* i. *tab.* 9. *fig.* 2.
	Filiformis.	*Ibid. tab.* 17. *fig.* 2.
	Minervæ.	*Ibid. p.* 36.
	Cinereus.	*Ibid. p.* 37.
	Mucofus.	*Ibid. tab.* 23. *fig.* 1.
	Cærulefcens.	*Ibid. tab.* 20. *fig.* 2.
VII.		
ANGUIS.	Meleagris.	*Seb. Muf.* ii. *tab.* 21. *fig.* 4.
	Scytale.	*Ibid. tab.* 2. *fig.* 1. 4.
	Ater.	*Ibid. tab.* 73. *fig.* 3.
VIII.		
CÆCILIA.	Tentaculata.	*Ibid. tab.* 25. *fig.* 2.
	Glutinofa.	*Muf. Ad. Fr.* i. *tab.* 4. *fig.* 1.

CLASSIS IV. PISCES.

ORDO I. BRANCHIOSTEGI.

GENUS.

I.

OSTRACION. TRIQUETER. - - - - - *Seb. Muf.* iii. *tab.* 24. *fig.* 6. 12.
Trigonus. - - - - - - - - - - *Artedi Gen.* 56. *fyn.* 85.
Bicaudalis. - - - - - - - - - - *Seb. Muf.* iii. *tab.* 24. *fig.* 3.
Tricornis.
Quadricornis. - - - - - - - - - *Edw. Glean. tab.* 284. *fig.* 1.
Cornutus. - - - - - - - - - - *Will. Ichth. t.* I. 13. *fig.* 1.
Tuberculatus. - - - - - - - - - - *Arted. Gen.* 55. *fyn.* 84.
Cubicus. - - - - - - - - - - *Seb. Muf.* iii. *tab.* 24. *fig.* 4. 5.

II.

TETRODON. Teftudineus. - - - - - - - - - *Amæn. Acad.* i. *tab.* 14. *fig.* 3.
Electricus. - - - - - - - - - *Act. Ang.* lxxvi. *p.* 382. *tab.* 13.
Oblongus. - - - - - - - - - *Bloch. Aufl. Fifch.* ii. *t.* 146. *fig.* 1.
Roftratus. - - - - - - - - - - - - - - - *Ibid. fig.* 2.
Hifpidus. - - - - - - - - - - *Amæn. Acad.* iv. *p.* 207. N° 23.

III.

SYNGNATHUS. Tetragonus. - - - - - - - *Bloch. Aufl. Fifch.* i. *t.* 121. *fig.* 1.
Hyppocampus. - - - - - - - - - - *Will. Ichth. tab.* I. 25.

IV.

PEGASUS. Draconis. - - - - - - - - - *Gron. Zooph. tab.* 12. *fig.* 2. 3.
Volans. - - - - - - - - - - - - - - *Muf. Ad.* ii. *p.* 56.
Natans. - - - - - - - - - *Bloch. Aufl. Fifch.* i. *t.* 121. *fig.* 2. 3.

V.

CENTRISCUS.	Scutatus. - - - - - - - - - -	*Gron. Muf.* ii. *tab.* 7. *fig.* 3.
	Valitaris. - - - - - - - -	*Pall. Spic. Zool.* viii. *tab.* 4. *fig.* 8.

VI.

BALISTES.	Tomentofus. - - - - - - - - - -	*Gron. Muf.* i. *tab.* 6. *fig.* 5.
	Verrucofus. - - - - - - - - -	*Muf. Ad. Fr.* i. *tab.* 27. *fig.* 4.
	Biaculeatus. - - - - - - - - -	*Will. Ichth. App. tab.* 10. *fig.* 2.
	Aculeatus. - - - - - - - - - -	*Seb. Muf.* iii. *tab.* 24. *fig.* 15.
	Vetula. - - - - - - - - - - - -	*Catefb. Carol.* ii. *tab.* 22.
	Caprifcus. - - - - - - - - - -	*Seb. Muf.* iii. *tab.* 24. *fig.* 16.
	Punctatus. - - - - - - - - - -	*Nieuhof. Ind.* ii. *p.* 275.
	Kleinii. - - - - - - - - -	*Klein. Miff. Pifc.* iii. *tab.* 3. *fig.* 12.

VII.

CYCLOPTERUS.	Lumpus. - - - - - - - -	β. γ. *Brit. Zool.* iii. *p.* 103. N° 1.
	Nudus. - - - - - - - - - -	*Muf. Ad. Fr.* i. *tab.* 27. *fig.* 1.

ORDO II. CHONDROPTERYGII.

VIII.

SQUALUS.	Catulus. - - - - - - - - - - -	*Brit. Zool.* iii. *p.* 90. N° 9.
	Tigrinus. - - - - - - - - - -	*Seb. Muf.* iii. *tab.* 34. *fig.* 1.
	Glaucus. - - - - - - - - - - -	*Brit. Zool.* iii. *p.* 84. N° 5.
	Canicula. - - - - - - - - - -	*Brit. Zool.* iii. *p.* 88. N° 8.
	Zygæna. - - - - - - - - - - - -	*Rondel. Pifc.* i. *p.* 389.
	Acanthias. - - - - - - - - - -	*Brit. Zool.* iii. *p.* 77. N° 2.
	Indicus. - - - - - - - - - - - -	*Gron. Muf.* i. N° 133.

IX.

RAJA.	Paftinaca. - - - - - - - - - -	*Brit. Zool.* iii. *p.* 71. N° 6.

ORDO III.

ORDO III. Apodes.

X.		
Muræna.	Colubrina.	*Pall. n. nord. Beytr.* ii. *t.* 2. *fig.* 3.
	Anguilla.	*Brit. Zool.* iii. *p.* 142. N° 12.
XI.		
Gymnotus.	Notopterus.	*Pall. Spicil. Zool.* vii. *tab.* 6. *fig.* 2.
XII.		
Trichiurus.	Indicus.	*Will. Ichth. App. tab.* 3. *fig.* 3.
XIII.		
Ophidium.	Aculeatum.	*Will. Ichth. App. tab.* 10. *fig.* 1.

ORDO IV. Jugulares.

XIV.		
Callionymus.	Ocellatus.	*Pall. Spic. Zool.* viii. *tab.* 4. *fig.* 13.
	Sagitta.	*Ibid. fig.* 4. 5.
XV.		
Gadus.	Lota.	*Brit. Zool.* iii. *p.* 163. N° 14.
XVI.		
Blennius.	Criſtatus.	*Gron. Muſ.* i. N° 75.
	Cornutus.	
	Faſciatus.	*Bloch. Auſl. Fiſch.* ii. *t.* 162. *fig.* 1.
	Superciliofus.	*Gron. Muſ.* ii. *tab.* 5. *fig.* 5.
	Muſtelaris.	

XVII. Kurtus.

XVII. KURTUS.	Indicus. - - - - - - - - - - -	*Bloch. Ausl. Fisch.* ii. *tab.* 169.

ORDO V. THORACICI.

XVIII. ECHENEIS.	Neucrates. - - - - - - - - - - -	*Seb. Mus.* iii. *tab.* 33. *fig.* 2.
XIX. CORYPHÆNA.	Pentadactyla. - - - - - - - - - -	*Bloch. Ausl. Fisch.* ii. *t.* 173.
	Fasciolata. - - - - - - - -	*Pall. Spicil. Zool.* viii. *tab.* 3. *fig.* 2.
	Velifera. - - - - - - - - - - - - - - - - -	*Ibid. fig.* 1.
XX. GOBIUS.	Schlosseri. - - - - - - - - - - - - - -	*Ibid. tab.* 1. *fig.* 1. 4.
	Bodærti. - - - - - - - - - - - - - -	*Ibid. tab.* 2. *fig.* 4. 5.
	Cyprinoides. - - - - - - - - - - - -	*Ibid. tab.* 1. *fig.* 5.
XXI. COTTUS.	Grunniens. - - - - - - - - - - -	*Seb. Mus.* iii. *tab.* 23. *fig.* 4.
	Scaber. - - - - - - - - - - - -	*Bloch. Ausl. Fisch.* ii. *tab.* 180.
	Monopterigius. - - - - -	*Bloch. Ausl. Fisch.* ii. *t.* 178. *fig.* 1. 2.
XXII. SCORPÆNA.	Horrida. - - - - - - - - -	*Gron. Zooph. tab.* 11. 12. 13. *fig.* 1.
	Volitans. - - - - - - - - - - -	*Will. Ichth. App. tab.* 2. *fig.* 3.
	Antennata. - - - - - - - - - -	*Bloch. Ausl. Fisch.* iii. *t.* 185.
	Didactyla. - - - - - - - -	*Pall. Spic. Zool.* vii. *tab.* 4. *fig.* 1. 3.
XXIII. ZEUS.	Insidiator. - - - - - - -	*Bloch. Ausl. Fisch.* iii. *tab.* 192. *fig.* 2. 3.
	Gallus. - - - - - - - - - - - - -	*Seb. Mus.* iii. *tab.* 26. *fig.* 34.
	Ciliaris. - - - - - - - - - - - - -	*Bloch. Ausl. Fisch. tab.* 191.

XXIV.		
PLEURONECTES.	Tricodactylus.	*Art. Gen.* 18. *ſyn.* 33. *ſp.* 60.
	Zebra.	*Bloch. Auſf. Fiſch.* iii. *tab.* 181.
XXV.		
CHÆTODON.	Caneſcens.	*Seb. Muſ.* iii. *tab.* 25. *fig.* 7.
	Acuminatus.	*Muſ. Ad. Fr.* i. *tab.* 33. *fig.* 3.
	Pinnatus.	*Ibid. fig.* 6.
	Cornutus.	*Seb. Muſ.* iii. *tab.* 25. *fig.* 6.
	Argenteus.	*Amœn. Acad.* iv. *p.* 249.
	Roſtratus.	*Ibid. fig.* 17.
	Orbis.	*Bloch. Auſf. Fiſch.* iii. *tab.* 102. *fig.* 2.
	Nigricans.	*Act. Angl.* 1784. ii. *tab.* 12.
	Lineatus.	*Seb. Muſ. tab.* 25. *fig.* 1.
	Trioſtegus.	*Brouſſonet Ichth. Dec.* i. *t.* 4.
	Macrolepidotus.	*Seb. Muſ.* iii. *t.* 25. *f.* 8.
	Argus.	*Will. Ichth. App. p.* 2. *t.* 2. *f.* 2.
	Striatus.	*Seb. Muſ.* iii. *tab.* 25. *fig.* 9.
	Arcuanus.	*Ibid. tab.* 26. *fig.* 23.
	Vagabundus.	*Ibid. tab.* 5. *fig.* 18.
	Ciliaris.	*Edw. Glean. tab.* 283. *fig.* 4.
	Saxatilis.	*Bloch. Auſf. Fiſch.* iii. *t.* 206. *fig.* 2.
	Rotundus.	*Muſ. Ad. Fr.* i. *p.* 64.
	Lanceolatus.	*Edw. Av. tab.* 210.
	Dux.	*Bloch. Auſf. Fiſch.* iii. *tab.* 195.
	Pavo.	*Ibid. tab.* 198. *fig.* 1.
	Veſpertilio.	*Ibid. tab.* 199. *fig.* 2.
	Unimaculatus.	*Ibid. tab.* 201. *fig.* 1.
	Bicolor.	*Ibid. tab.* 206. *fig.* 1.
	Ocellatus.	*Ibid. tab.* 211. *fig.* 2.
	Bengalenſis	*Ibid. tab.* 213. *fig.* 2.
	Octofaſciatus.	*Ibid. tab.* 215. *fig.* 1.
	Annularis.	*Ibid. tab.* 215. *fig.* 2.
	Faber.	*Ibid. tab.* 212. *fig.* 2.
	Teira.	*Ibid. tab.* 199. *fig.* 1. *Forſk. Fn. Arab. p.* 60. N° 82.

XXVI. SPARUS.

XXVI. SPARUS.	Insidiator.	*Pall. Spic. Zool. tab.* 5. *fig.* 1.
	Palpebratus.	*Pall. n. nord. Beytr.* ii. *t.* 4. *fig.* 1. 2.
	Spinus.	*Mus. Ad. Fr.* ii. *p.* 74 *.
XXVII. SCARUS.	Schlosseri.	*Pall. Spic. Zool.* viii. *p.* 41.
XXVIII. LABRUS.	Lunaris.	*Gron. Mus.* ii. *tab.* 6. *fig.* 2.
	Trichopterus.	*Pall. Spic. Zool.* viii. *p.* 45.
	Zeylanicus.	*Ind. Zool. tab.* 13. *fig.* 3.
	Ferrugineus.	
	Paroticus.	*Mus. Ad. Fr.* ii. *p.* 76.
	Linearis.	*Amœn. Acad.* i. *p.* 315.
XXIX. PERCA.	Polymna.	*Seb. Mus.* iii. *tab.* 26. *f.* 20. 24.
	Cottoides.	*Mus. Ad. Fr.* ii. *p.* 84.
	Stigma.	
	Radula.	*Amœn. Acad.* i. *p.* 313.
XXX. TRIGLA.	Minuta.	

ORDO VI. ABDOMINALES.

XXXI. SILURUS.	Ascita.	*Mus. Ad. Fr.* i. *p.* 79. *t.* 30. *fig.* 2.
	Costatus.	*Gron. Mus.* ii. *tab.* 5. *fig.* 1. 2.
XXXII. TEUTHIS.	Hepatus.	*Catesb. Carol.* ii. *tab.* 1. *fig.* 1.
	Java.	*Valent. Ind.* iii. *p.* 339. *fig.* 410.

XXXIII.		
SALMO.	Gasteropelecus. - - - - -	*Pall. Spic. Zool.* viii. *t.* 3. *fig.* 4. 5.
	Anostomus. - - - - - - - - -	*Gron. Mus.* ii. *tab.* 7. *fig.* 2.
XXXIV.		
FISTULARIA.	Chinensis. - - - - - - - - - - -	*Pet. Gaz. tab.* 68. *fig.* 1.
	Paradoxa. - - - - - - -	*Pall. Spic. Zool.* viii. *tab.* 4. *fig.* 6.
XXXV.		
ESOX.	Brasiliensis. - - - - - - - - -	*Brown Jam. tab.* 45. *fig.* 2.
	Gymnocephalus.	
XXXVI.		
POLYNEMUS.	Paradiseus. - - - - - - - - - - -	*Edw. Av. tab.* 208.
XXXVII.		
CLUPEA.	Thrissa. - - - - - - - - - - -	*Brousson. Ichth.* i. *tab.* 10.
	Mystus. - - - - - - - - -	*Amæn. Acad.* v. *tab.* . *fig.* 12.
XXXVIII.		
CYPRINUS.	Tinca. - - -	*Brit. Zool.* iii. *p.* 306. N° 3. *Will. Ichth. t.* 2. 5.

CLASSIS V. Insecta.

ORDO I. Eleuterata.

Lucanus.	Alces.	*Fab. Sp. Inf.*	N° 1.	*Petiv. Gazoph.*	*tab.* 47. *f.* 15.
	Gazella.	*Fab. Mantiss. p.* 1.		*Oliv. Coleopt.* (Lucan.)	*pl.* 4. *f.* 13. a. b.
	Lama.				*pl.* 3. *f.* 8.
	Carinatus.	*Lin. S. N.*	N° 5.		
Scarabæus.	Alcides.	*Fab. Sp. Inf.*	N° 2.	*Oliv. Col.* (Scar.)	*pl.* 1. *f.* 2.
	Gideon. Lin.		3.		*pl.* 11. *f.* 102.
	Centaurus.		4.		*pl.* 11. *f.* 104.
	Oromedon.		5.		*pl.* 18. 165.
	Ægeon.		6.		*pl.* 26. *f.* 119.
	Dichotomus. Lin.		9.		*pl.* 17. *f.* 156.
	Claviger.		10.		*pl.* 5. *f.* 40. a. β.
	Pan.		12.		*pl.* 5. *f.* 35. *pl.* 23. *f.* 30. β.
	Simson.		19.		*pl.* 15. *f.* 142.
	Geryon.		25.		*pl.* 24. *f.* 208.
	Quadrispinosus.		36.		*pl.* 19. *f.* 179.
	Quadridens.		37.		*pl.* 12. *f.* 108. a. b.
	Enema.	*Fab. Mant. Inf.*	N° 12.		
	Rhinoceros. L.	*Fab. Sp. Inf.*	N° 40.		*pl.* 18. *f.* 166.
	Coronatus.		N° 47.		*pl.* 12. *f.* 110.

Hircus.	*Fab. Sp. Inſ.* N°	52.		
Piceus.		55.	*Oliv. Col.* (Scar.)	*pl.* 24. *f.* 211.
Aygulus.		57.		*pl.* 13. *f.* 120. & *pl.* 4. *f.* 28. a. b.
Analis.	*Fab. Mant. Inſ.*	64.		
Unifaſciatus.	*Gmel. Lin.* N°	182.	*Schall. Hall. Naturf.*	1. *p.* 240.
Scaber. L.	*Fab. Spec. Inſ.*	72.	*Oliv. Col.*	*pl.* 23. *f.* 1. c.
Pygmæus.	*Gmel. Lin.*	186.	*Sch. H. Nat.*	*f.* 1. *p.* 239.
Longimanus. L.	*Fab. Sp. Inſ.*	73.	*Oliv. Col.*	*pl.* 4. *f.* 27.
Veter.	*Mant. App. p.*	377.		
Barbatus.	*Spec. Inſ.* N°	83.		
Marginellus.		88.		*pl.* 13. *f.* 116. a. b.
Sabæus.		99.		*pl.* 9. *f.* 85.
Pithecius.		102.		*pl.* 9. *f.* 73.
Seniculus.		103.		*pl.* 7. *f.* 56. a. b.
Ammon.		105.		*pl.* 12. *f.* 111.
Rhadamiſtus.		109.		*pl.* 14. *f.* 136. a. b.
Lar.	*Mantiſſ. Inſ.*	124.		
Bifaſciatus.	*Spec. Inſ.*	111.		*pl.* 13. *f.* 119. a. b.
Capucinus.		113.		*pl.* 2. *f.* 12. *pl.* 25. *f.* 12. b.
Boas.	*Mant. Inſ.*	129.		
Bonaſus.	*Spec. Inſ.*	114.		*pl.* 6. *f.* 43. a—c.
Bucephalus.		117.		*pl.* 4. *f.* 26. *pl.* 10. *f.* 92. b.
Lancifer. L.		119.		*pl.* 4. *f.* 32.
Spinifey.		131.		*pl.* 12. *f.* 112.
Fricator.	*Mant. Inſ.*	140.		
Miliaris.	*Sp. Inſ.*	141.		*pl.* 18. *f.* 164.
Koenigii.		145.		*pl.* 9. *f.* 77.
Pallipes.		153.		

Æneus.

	Æneus.	*Sp. Inſ.* 156. *Oliv. Coleop.* (Scar.)	*pl.* 14. *f.* 128. a. b.
	Catta.	*Fab. Mant.* N° 115.	*pl.* 23. *f.* 201.
	Augias.		*pl.* 24. *f.* 212.
	Melampus.		*pl.* 17. *f.* 159.
	Tullius.		*pl.* 19 *f.* 88. b. & *pl.* 11. *f.* 98.
	Heſperus.		*pl.* 14. *f.* 129.
	Sinuatus.		*pl.* 21. *f.* 189. & *pl.* 10. *f.* 93.
	Erraticus.	*Lin. S. Nat.* N° 29. *Faun. Suec.* N° 383.	
TROX.	Horridus.	*Fab. Sp. Inſ.* N° 3. *Oliv. Col.* (Trox.)	*pl.* 1. *f.* 2.
MELOLONTHA.	Serrata.	2. *Oliv. Col.* (Melol.)	*pl.* 1. *f.* 5.
	Lanigera.	10.	*pl.* 4. *f.* 39. a. b.
	Glabrata.	12.	*pl.* 9. *f.* 80.
	Dorſalis.	17.	
	Ruficollis.	24.	*pl.* 9. *f.* 111.
	Erythrocephala.	28.	*pl.* 7. *f.* 80.
	Rauca.	37.	*pl.* 6. *f.* 62.
	Ferruginea.	38.	*pl.* 7. *f.* 82.
	Proboſcidea.	49.	*pl.* 8. *f.* 96.
	Podagrica.	52.	*pl.* 5. *f.* 51.
	Mutabilis.	60.	*pl.* 3. *f.* 24.
	Vittata.	74.	*pl.* 8. *f.* 94.
	Candida.	N° 8.	*pl.* 8. *f.* 98.
	Femoralis.	41.	*pl.* 9. *f.* 110.
	Pubeſcens.	57.	*pl.* 6. *f.* 71.
	Unicolor.	*Gmel. Lin.* 313. *Fueſl. Arc. Inſ.* 7.	*p.* 43. *f.* 5.
	Ciliatus.	314.	*f.* 6.
	Sepicola.	*Lin. S. Nat.* 55. *Muſ. Lud. Ulr.* 24.	

Syriacus.

Syriacus. - *Lin. S. Nat.* N° 56. *Muf. Lud. Ulr.* - 25.
Leei. - - - *Gmel. Lin.* 427. *N. Act. Stockh.* 8. 1787. 3. N° 3. 4.

TRICHIUS. Indus. - - *Fab. Sp. Inf.* N° 2. *Oliv. Col.* (Ceton.) *pl.* 6. *f.* 40.
Viridulus. - - - - - - - 6. - - - - - - *pl.* 6. *f.* 86.

CETONIA. Chinenfis. - - - - - - - 2. - - - - - - *pl.* 2. *f.* 5. a. b.
Nigrita. - - - - - - - 3. - - - - - - *pl.* 10. *f.* 92.
Splendida. - - - - - - 31. - - - - - - *pl.* 4. *f.* 21.
Elegans. - - - - - - - 32. - - - - - - *pl.* 4. *f.* 25.
Aurichalcea. - - - - - - 43. - - - - - - *pl.* 9. *f.* 78.
Orichalca. *Lin. S. N.* iii. *App. p.* 224.
Maculata. - *Fab. Sp. Inf.* N° 46. - - - - - - *pl.* 7. *f.* 66.
Verficolor. - - - - - - 52. - - - - - - *pl.* 4. *f.* 23.
Variegata. - - - - - - 55. - - - - - - *pl.* 5. *f.* 31. b. & 30.
Quadripunctata. *Fab. Mant.* N° 12. - - - - - - *pl.* 10. *f.* 93.
Capucina. - - - - - - 16.
Ephippium. - - - - - - 31. *Drur. Inf.* - - 3. *pl.* 44. *f.* 3.
Bifida. - - - - - - - - *Oliv. Col.* (Cet.) N° 43. *pl.* 2. *f.* 9.
Crucifera. - - - - - - - - - - - - - - 44. *pl.* 5. *f.* 29.
Impreffa. - - - - - - - - - - - - - - 45. *pl.* 8. *f.* 71.
Cærulea. - - - - - - - - - - - - - - 55. *pl.* 5. *f.* 31. a.
Cærulea. - - *Gmel. Lin.* 382. *Fueſl. Arch. Inf.* - 4. *tab.* 19. *f.* 30.
Bimucronata. - - - - 384. *Pall. Ic. Inf. Roff.* 1. *tab.* A. *f.* 13.

HISTER. Maximus. - *Lin. S. Nat.* N° 1. *Oliv. Col.* (Hift.) - *pl.* 1. *f.* 2.
Major. L. - *Fab. Spec. Inf.* N° 2. - - - - - - *pl.* 1. *f.* 4. a. b.

APATE. Capucinus. - - - - - - 4. *Sch. El.* - - - - *t.* 28.

DERMESTES.	Lardarius. L. - *Fab. Spec. Inf.* 1.	*Schæf. Ic.* - - -	*pl.* 42. *f.* 3.
	Pellio. - - - - - - - - 5.	- - - - - -	*pl.* 42. *f.* 4.
	Ruficollis. - - - - - - 15.	*Thunb. N. Sp. Inf.*	1. *p.* 8. *f.* 7.
	Marginatus. - - *Gmel. Lin.* 44.	- - - - - -	*pl.* 7. *f.* 6.
	Piceus. - - - - - - - 45.	- - - - - -	*p.* 8.
	Viridis. - - - - - - - - 48.	- - - - - -	*p.* 9.

BRUCHUS.	Cacao. - - - - - - N° 6.
	Theobromæ. L. - - - - - 7.
	Analis. - - - - - - - - 9.
	Abdominalis - - - - - 13.

TRITOMA. Vittata. - - *Fab. Mant.* N° 4.

HISPA. Bihamata. - *Lin. S. Nat.* N° 3.

SILPHA. Indica. L. - *Fab. Sp. Inf.* N° 3. *Muf. Lud. Ulr.* - 38.

OPATRUM. Cinereum. - - *Gmel. Lin.* 11. *Fuefl. Arch. Inf.* - 4. *tab.* 21. A. a.

COCCINELLA.	Dimidiata. - *Fab. Sp. Inf.* N° 5.		
	Cingulata. - *Fab. Mant.* N° 24.		
	Sexmaculata. - *Spec. Inf.* N° 20.		
	Septempunctata. L. - - 21.	*Schæf. Ic.* - - -	*tab.* 9. *f.* 7.
	Centumpunctata. *Gmel. Lin.* 118.	*Fuefl. Arch. Inf.* -	4. *tab.* 22. *f.* 13.
	Tranfverfalis. *Fab. Spec. Inf.* 24.		
	Sparfa. - - - *Gmel. Lin.* 120.	- - - - - -	7. *tab.* 43. *f.* 11.
	28-punctata. - - - - 48.		
	Minuta. - - - - - - - 54.	*Thunb. N. Sp. Inf.*	1. *p.* 11.

CASSIDA.

CASSIDA. 8-punctata. - *Fab. Mant.* N° 18.
Marginata. L. - *Sp. Inf.* N° 25. *Naturforsch.* - N° 9. *t.* 2.
Dorsata. - - - *Mantiss.* 33.
Bicornis. L. - - *Sp. Inf.* 29. *Amæn. Ac.* - - 6. *p.* 393. 9.
Spinifex. L. - - - - - - 31. - - - - - - *p.* 392. 7.
Trifasciata. - - - *Mant.* 46.
Annulata. - - - *Spec. Inf.* 39. *Naturf.* - - - 9. *t.* 2. *f.* 6.
Bipunctata. L. - - - - - 49.
Alatrata. - *Lin. S. Nat.* N° 18.
Angustata. - *Gmel. Lin.* N° 31.

ALURNUS. Femoratus. - *Fab. Sp. Inf.* N° 2. *Drur. Inf.* - - 2. *tab.* 34. *f.* 5.

CHRYSOMELA. 14-punctata. L. - - - - - 13.
Fervide. - - - - - - - 22.
Undulata. L. - - - - - 41. *Amæn. Ac.* - - 6. *p.* 393. 14.
Nitida. - - - *Mant.* N° 64.
Cruenta. - - - *Spec. Inf.* 82.
Sternicornis. - *Gmel. Lin.* 147. *Schal. Hall. Nat.* 1. *t.* 1. *f.* 1.
Gigas. - - - - - - 153. *Fuesl. Arch. Inf.* - 4. *t.* 23. *f.* 2.
Indica. - - - - - - - 155. - - - - - - *f.* 5.
Malaccensis. - - - - - 249. *Horn. Sbr. Berl. Nat.* 8. *t.* 1. *f.* 9.
Fascicornis. (Altica.) - - 66. - - - - - - - *f.* 1.

CRYPTOCEPHALUS. Koenigii. - *Fab. Sp. Inf.* 45.
Martinius. - *Gmel. Lin.* N° 74. *Schal. Hall. Nat.* 1. *p.* 278.
Peregrinus. - - - - - - 77. *Fuesl. Arch. Inf.* - 4. *t.* 23. *f.* 25.
Multicolor. - - - - - 246. *Horn. Sbr. Berl. Nat.* 8. *t.* 1. *f.* 6.
Sumatranus. - - - - - 247. - - - - - - *f.* 4.
Coffeæ. - - - - - - - 248. - - - - - - *f.* 7.
Orientalis. - - - - - - 249. - - - - - - *f.* 3.
Bataviensis. - - - - - 250. - - - - - - *f.* 12.
Javanus. - - - - - - - 251. - - - - - - *f.* 2. 5. 8. 11.

CRITELA.

CISTELA.	Analis. - - - *Fab. Sp. Inf.* 8.		
CRIOCERIS.	Cincta. - - - - - - - 5.		
	Palliata. - - - - - - - 6.	*Act. Hall.* - -	1. *p.* 279.
	Picta. - - - - *Mantiss.* 12.		
	Testacea. - - - - - - - 20.		
	4-pustulata. - - - - - - 23.		
	Impressa. - - - - - - - 24.		
	Abdominalis. - *Gmel. Lin.* 130.		
	Ochracea. - - - - - - 180.	*Fuesl. Arch. Inf.* -	7. *t.* 44. *f.* 9. p. q.
EROTYLUS.	Giganteus. L. *Fab. Sp. Inf.* N° 1.	*De Geer, Inf.* -	5. *tab.* 16. *f.* 8.
	Longimanus. - *Mant.* N° 11.		
LAGRIA.	Abdominalis. - *Fab. Mant.* N° 14.		
	Inda. - - *Lin. S. Nat.* N° 121.	*Muf. Lud. Ulr.* -	41.
CURCULIO.	Palmarum. L. - *Sp. Inf.* N° 1.	*Oliv. Col.* (Curc.) -	*pl.* 2. *f.* 16.
	Indus. L. - - - - - - 5.	*De Geer, Inf.* -	5. *pl.* 15. *f.* 22.
	Paganus. - - - - - - - 6.		
	Hemipterus. L. - - - - - 8.	- - - - - -	*pl.* 15. *f.* 25.
	Melanocardius. L. - - - 10.	*Sulz. Inf.* - -	4. *tab.* 4. *f.* 11.
	Barbirostris. - - - - - - 65.	*Seb. Muf.* - -	4. *tab.* 95. *f.* 5.
	Frigidus. *Fab. Mant. App. p.* 381.		
	Mucoreus. L. *Fab. Sp. Inf.* N° 74.	*Muf. Lud. Ulr.* -	53.
	Pusio. L. - - - - - - 75.	- - - - -	46.
	Stigma. L. - - - - - - 79.	- - - - -	48.
	Hebes. - - - - - - - 80.		
	Annulatus. L. - - - - - 81.	- - - - -	51.
	Reticulatus. - - - - - - 85.		
	Stultus. - - *Mant.* N° 117.		
	Anchoraco. L. - *Spec. Inf.* 118.	*De Geer, Inf.* -	5. *tab.* 15. *f.* 4.

	Argyreus. L.	- *Spec. Inſ.* 128.	*Muſ. Lud. Ulr.*	54.
	Curvipes.	- - - *Mant.* 183.		
	Lacerta.	- - - *Spec. Inſ.* 161.		
	Frigidus.	- *Mant. App. p.* 381.		
	Emeritus. L.	- *Spec. Inſ.* 190.	- - - - -	56.
	Cinnamomi.	- *Gmel. Lin.* 275.	*Fueſl. Arch. Inſ.* -	5. *t.* 24. *f.* 20. h. i.
	Globoſus.	- *Fab. Sp. Inſ.* N° 193.	*Drur. Inſ.* - -	1. *pl.* 32. *f.* 4.
	Apterus. L.	- - - - - 206.	*De Geer. Inſ.* -	5. *tab.* 16. *f.* 1.
	Viridanus.	- - - - - - 219.		
ATTELABUS.	Indicus.	- - - *Mant.* N° 5.	*Thunb. N. Spec. Inſ.*	3. *pl.* 68. *f.* 81.
	Cyaneus.	- - - - - - - 15.		
CLERUS.	Apiarius. L.	*Fab. Sp. Inſ.* N° 9.	*Schæf. Ic.* - - -	*pl.* 48. *f.* 11.
	Cyaneus.	- - - *Mant.* N° 15.		
PRIONUS.	Trochlearis.	*Lin. S. Nat. p.* 622.		
	Armillatus. L.	*Fab. Sp. Inſ.* N° 21.	*Oliv. Col.* (Prion.)	*pl.* 5. *f.* 17.
	Roſtratus.	- - - *Mant.* N° 3.		
	Spinoſus.	- - - - - - - 26.		
CERAMBYX.	Gigas.	- - *Fab. Mant.* N° 20.		
	Faſciatus.	- - *Spec. Inſ.* N° 23.		
	Barbicornis. L.	- - - - - 24.	*Muſ. L. Ulr.* -	68.
	Rugicollis.	- - - *Mantiſſ.* 40.		
	Holoſericeus	- - - - - - 45.		
	Longicollis	- - - - - - 46.		
	Sentis.	- *Lin. S. Nat. p.* 626. 23.		
	Ferrugineus.	- - - - - 25.		
	Platypus.	- *Gmel. Lin.* N° 132.	*De Geer, Inſ.* -	7. *t.* 49. *f.* 3.

LAMIA.	Vaginator. - *Fab. Mant.* N° 8.			
	Grisator. - - - - - - - 12.			
	Nigricornis. - - *Spec. Inf.* 10.			
	Ariolator. - - - - - - 14.			
	Reticulator. - - - - - 16.			
	Rotator. - - - - - - - 32.			
	Lusia. - - *Fab. Mant.* N° 35.			
	Molitor. - - - *Spec. Inf.* 42.			
	Rubus. L. - - - - - - 44.	*De Geer, Inf.* -	5. *t.* 13. *f.* 16.	
	Scabrator. - - - - - 46.			
	Sentis. - - *Lin. S. Nat.* N° 23.			
	Ferrugineus. - - - - - 25.	*Mus. Lud. Ulr.* -	70.	
	Depressus. - - - - - 26.	*Schr. Inf.* - -	8. *f.* 10.	
STENOCORUS.	Cyaneus. - *Fab. Spec. Inf.* N° 2.	*Forst. Cent. Inf.*	40. (palliatus.)	
	Rusticus. - - - - - - - 19.			
SAPERDA.	Vittata. - - - - - - - 11.			
CALLIDIUM.	Barbatum. - - - - - - 12.			
	Compressum. - - *Mant.* 21.			
	Glaucum. - - - *Spec. Inf.* 41.			
	Annulare. - - - *Mant.* 59.			
	Venustum. - - *Gmel. Lin.* 298.	*Fuesl. Arch. Inf.* -	5. *t.* 26. *f.* 12.	
	Indicum. - - - - - - 299.	- - - - - -	*f.* 16.	
LEPTURA.	Linearis. - *Lin. S. Nat.* N° 25.	*Mus. Lud. Ulr.* -	77.	
LAMPYRIS.	Cincta. - - - *Fab. Sp. Inf.* 6.			
	Depressa - - - - - - 18.			
	Compressa. - *Gmel. Lin.* N° 23.	*Thunb. N. Sp. Inf.*	4. *p.* 80.	

PYROCHROA. Nigripes. - - - - *Mantiss.* 5.

LYMEXYLON. Testaceum. *Fab. Spec. Inf.* N° 1.

CUCUJUS. Rufus. - - *Gmel. Lin.* N° 10. *Swed. Act. Stock.* - 8. N° 3. 21.

CANTHARIS. Melanocephala. *Fab. Spec. Inf.* 13.
Tropica. - *Lin. S. Nat.* N° 19. *Gron. Zooph.* - 515. *t.* 14. *f.* 7.

ELATER. Flabellicornis. L. *Fab. Sp. Inf.* N° 1. *Dr. Inf.* - - - 3. *pl.* 47. *f.* 1.?
Speciosus. L. - - - - - - 2.
Luridus. - - - - - - - 3.
Fuscipes. - - - - - - - 9.
Melanocephalus. - - - 38.
Notatus. - - - - - - - 45.
Pallipes. - *Fab. Inf. Mant.* 46.

BUPRESTIS. Gigantea. L. - - - - - - 3. *Petiv. Gaz.* - - *t.* 147. *f.* 16. 17.
Vittata. - - - - - - - - 4.
Ignita, L. - - - - - - 12. - - - - - - *t.* 20. *f.* 8.
Ænea. - - - - - - - - 15.
Sternicornis. L. - - - - - 17. *Grew, Mus.* - - *t.* 13.
Chrysis. L. - - - - - - 18. *De Geer, Inf.* - 4. *t.* 17. *f.* 25.
Fulminans. - - *Mantiss.* 29.
Impressa. - - - *Spec. Inf.* 27.
Scabra. - - - - - - - 30.
Plebeia. - - - - - - - 41.
Impressa. - - - *Mant.* 61.
Bimaculata. - - *Spec. Inf.* 45. *Sulz. Inf.* - - 57. *t.* 6. *f.* 15.
4-maculata. - - - - - - 46.

Tristis.

Triftis. L. - *Fab. Sp. Inf.* N° 47. *Muf. Lud. Ulr.* - 93.
Nobilis. L. - - - - - - 49.
Stricta. - - *Lin. S. Nat.* N° 4. - - - - 87.

CICINDELA. Longicollis. - *Fab. Mantiff.* N° 1.
Groffa. - - - *Spec. Inf.* N° 1.
Cyanea. - - - - *Mant.* 2.
Bicolor. - - - - *Spec. Inf.* 2.
Sexpunctata. - - - - - - 14.
4-lineata. - - - - - - - 15.
Biramofa. - - - *Mantiff.* 20. *Thunb. N. Sp. Inf.* 1. *pl.* 26. *f.* 40.
Catena. - - - *Spec. Inf.* 18.

HYDROPHILUS. Olivaceus. - - - - - 2.

DYTISCUS. Limbatus. - - - *Sp. Inf.* 5.
Ruficollis. - - - *Mant.* N° 6.
Fafciatus. - - *Fab. Sp. Inf.* 7.
Vittatus. - - - *Spec. Inf.* 10.
Grifeus. - - - - - - - 12.
Aciculatus. - - *Gmel. Lin.* 64. *Fueſl. Arch. Inf.* - 5. *p.* 123. N° 4.
Zeylanicus. - - - - - - 83. *Gron. Muf.* - - 2. *p.* 164. N° 552.

GYRINUS. Spinofus. - - - - - - 4.

CARABUS. 6-guttatus. - - - - - - 6.
Reflexus. - - - - - - 20.
Angulatus. - *Fab. Spec. Inf.* 21.
Levigatus. - - - - - - 28.
Attelaboides. - - - - - 30.
Trilineatus. - - - - - - 31.

Bimaculatus.

Bimaculatus. L. *Fab. Spec. Inſ.* 45. *Sulz. H. Inſ.* - - *t.* 7. *f.* 5.
Cinctus. - - - - - - 62.
Flexuoſus. - - - - - - 66.
Indicus. - - *Gmel. Lin.* 153. *Fueſl. Arch. Inſ.* - 6. *t.* 29. *f.* 11.
Splendidus. - - - - - - 154. - - - - - - *p.* 138. N° 41.
Marginellus. - - - - - 155. - - - - - - *p.* 138. N° 42.

PIMELIA. Striata. - - - - - - - - 1.
Gibba. - - - - - *Mantiſſ.* 3.
Faſciata. - - - - *Spec.* 18.

SCARITES. Bucephalus. - *Gmel. Lin.* N° 20. - - - - - - *t.* 29. *f.* 16. 1.

BLAPS. Striata. - - *Fab. Sp. Inſ.* N° 5.
Crenata. - - - - - - - 6.

TENEBRIO. Laminatus. - - - *Mantiſſ.* 1.
Punctulatus. - - - - - - 2.
Abbreviatus. - - *Spec. Inſ.* 6.

HELOPS. Maura. - - - - - - - - 5.
Dentipes. - - - - - - - 12.

MYLABRIS. Faſciata. - - - - - - - 1.
Algirica. L. - - - - - - 3.
Indica. - - - *Gmel. Lin.* 16. - - - - - - 6. *t.* 30. *f.* 6.
Undulata. - - - - - - 18. - - - - - - 8. *t.* 48. *f.* 3.
Biſaſciata. - - - - - - 21. - - - - - - *t.* 48. *f.* 2.

LYTTA.

LYTTA.	Syriaca. L.	*Fab. Sp. Inf.* 3. *Fuefl. Arch. Inf.* -	6. *t.* 30. *f.* 1.
	Ruficollis. - -	*Gmel. Lin.* 13. - - - - - -	8. *t.* 48. *f.* 4.

STAPHYLINUS. Aureus. - - - *Mantiff.* 1.

ORDO II. ULONATA.

BLATTA.	Gigantea. L.	*Fab. Sp. Inf.* N° 1. *Drur. Inf.* - -	2. *t.* 36. *f.* 2.
	Indica. - - - - - - -	8.	
	Petiveriana. - - - - -	13. *Petiv. Gaz.* - -	*t.* 71. *f.* 1.
	Orientalis. L. - - - -	14. *Schæf. Ic.* - - -	*t.* 88. *f.* 2. 3.
	Ruficollis. - - -	*Mantiff.* 22.	
	Aterrima. - -	*Gmel. Lin.* 32. *Fuefl. Arch. Inf.* -	8. *t.* 49. *f.* 9.

MANTIS.	Gigas. L. -	*Fab. Spec. Inf.* 1. *Petiv. Gaz.* - -	*t.* 60. *f.* 2.
	Necydaloides. L. - - -	2. *Roef.* 2. *Gryl.* - -	*t.* 19.
	Atrophica. - - - - - -	3. *Pall. Spic. fafc.* -	9. *t.* 5. *f.* 1.
	Bifpinofa. - - - - - - -	4.	
	Linearis. - - - -	*Mant.* 9.	
	Gongyloides. L. -	*Sp. Inf.* 8. *Drur. Inf.* - -	1. *t.* 36. *f.* 2.
	Pauperata. - - - - - -	9.	
	Strumaria. L. - - - -	11. *Roef. Inf.* 2. *Gryll.*	*t.* 2.
	Tricolor. L. - - - - -	12. *Muf. Lud. Ulr.* 117.	
	Cancellata. - - - . -	13.	
	Siccifolia. L. - - - - -	14. *Roef. Inf.* 2. *Gryll.*	*t.* 17.
	Pectinicornis. L. - - -	15. *Drur. Inf.* - -	1. *t.* 50. *f.* 1.
	Urbana. - - - - - - -	26.	
	Pulchra. - - -	*Mantiff.* 34.	

ACHETA.	Gryllotalpa. - -	*Spec. Inf.* 1. *Roef. Inf.* 2. *Gryll.*	*t.* 14. 15.

Monftrofa,

Monstrosa. - *Fab. Sp. Inf.* N° 2. *Drur. Inf.* - - 2. *t.* 42. *f.* 1.
Orientalis. - - - - - - 7.

Locusta. Citrifolia. L. - - - - - - 1. *Roes. Inf.* 2. *Gryll.* *t.* 16. *f.* 1.
Elongata. L. - - - - - 10. - - - - - - *t.* 18. *f.* 7.
Femorata. - - *Fab. Mant.* 12.
Ocellata. L. - - *Sp. Inf.* 12. *Seb. Mus.* - - 4. *t.* 73. *f.* 7. 8.
Triops. L. - - - - - - 16.
Coronata. L. - *Fab. Sp. Inf.* 17. *De Geer, Inf.* - 3. *t.* 38. *f.* 5.
Melanoptera. L. - - - 18.
Coriacea. L. - - - - 19. *Mus. Ad. Fr.* - 136.
Spinulosa. L. - - - - - 28. *Edw. Av.* - - 2. *t.* 285. *f.* 3. 4. 5.
Indica. - *Gmel. Lin.* N° 116. *Fuesl. Arch. Inf.* - 8. *t.* 53. *f.* 2.
Unicolor. - *Lin. S. Nat.* N° 3. *Mus. Lud. Ulr.* 119.
Carinata. - - - - - - - 6. - - - - - 122.
Lamellosa. - - - - - - 21. *Roes. Gryll.* - - *t.* 18. *f.* 7?
Rugosa. - - - - - - - 25. *Mus. Lud. Ulr.* 132.
Aquilina. - - - - - - 27. - - - - - 133.
Fastigiata. - - - - - - 29. - - - - - 135.

Gryllus. Succinctus. L. - - *Fab. Sp.* 2. *Amœn. Ac.* - - 6. *p.* 398. 36.
Reticulatus. - - - - - - 7.
Serripes. - - - *Mantiss.* 8.
Turcicus. - - - - - - 10.
Punctatus. - - - *Sp. Inf.* 14. *Drur. Inf.* - - 2. *t.* 41. *f.* 4.
Hæmatopus. L. - - - 16. *De Geer. Inf.* - 5. *t.* 40. *f.* 10.
Perspicillatus. L. - - - 50. *Amœn. Ac.* - - 6. *p.* 398. 34.

ORDO III. Synistata.

Monoculus. Polyphemus. L. *Fab. Sp. Inf.* N° 1. *Rumph. Mus.* - 21. *t.* 12.

Oniscus.

ONISCUS. Linearis. L. - *Fab. Sp. Inf.* N° 8. *Pall. Spic. fasc.* - 9. *t.* 4. *f.* 11.

SEMBLIS. Fuscata. - - - - - - - 4.

TERMES. Fatale. L. - - - - - - - - 1. *De Geer, Inf.* - 7. *t.* 37. *f.* 1. 2.

MYRMELEON. Pardalis. - - - - - - 2.
Punctatum. - - - *Mant.* 7.

ICHNEUMON. Pedator. - - - *Spec. Inf.* 52.
Polycerator. - - - - - 63.
Punctatus. - - - - - - 104.

SPHEX. Fervens. L. - - - - - - 12. *Mus. Lud. Ulr.* 406.
Erythrocephala. - - - - 14.
Argentata. - - - *Mantiss.* 6.
Maderaspatana. - *Spec. Inf.* 16.
Compressa. - - - - - - 19.
Ciliata. - - - - *Mantiss.* 24.
Vespiformis. *Fab. Sp. Inf.* N° 23.
Analis. - - - - - - - 27.
Affimilis. - - - *Mantiss.* 33.
Tropica. L. - - *Spec. Inf.* 37. - - - - - 408.
Maura. - - - - *Mantiss.* 38.
Aurata. - - - - - - - 45.
Nigrita. - - - *Spec. Inf.* 45.
Villosa. - - - - - - - 47.
Flava. - - - - - - - 48.
Flavicornis. - - - - - 50.
Indostana. - *Lin. S. Nat.* N° 7. - - - - - 407.
Indica. - - - - - - - - 26. - - - - - 408.

TIPHIA.	Collaris. - *Fab. Sp. Inf.* N° 8.		
	Dorsata. - - - *Mantiss.* 11.		
	Ruficornis. - - - - - - 12.		
SCOLIA.	4-pustulata. - - *Sp. Inf.* 13.		
CHRYSIS.	Splendida. - - - - - - 1.		
	Oculata - - - - - - - 4.		
BEMBEX.	Repanda. - - - *Mantiss.* 6.		
	Interrupta. - - - - - - 8.		
VESPA.	Cincta. - - *Fab. Sp. Inf.* N° 1.	*Sulz. Inf.* - - -	*t.* 27. *f.* 5.
	Cornuta. L. - - - *Sp. Inf.* 7.	*Drur. Inf.* - -	2. *t.* 48. *f.* 3.
	Calida. L. - - - - - - 23.		
	4-punctata - - - *Mantiss.* 55.		
	Hebræa. - - - - - - - 58.		
	Flavescens. - - - *Sp. Inf.* 50.		
	Petiolata. - - - - - - 56.		
	Esuriens. - - - *Mantiss.* 75.		
CRABRO.	Cornutus. - *Fab. Mant.* N° 3.		
	Repandus. - - - - - - 5.		
	Interruptus. - - - - - - 10.		
ANDRENA.	Cincta - - - - *Sp. Inf.* 8.		
	Zonata. L. - - - - - - 11.	*Mus. Lud. Ulr.*	415.
APIS.	Plumipes. - - - - - - 35.		

Bicolor.

	Bicolor.	*Sp. Inſ.* 55.	
	Villoſa.	56.	
	Florea.	*Mantiſſ.* 87.	
	Smaragdula.	91.	
	Cordata?	*Lin. S. Nat.* 15.	*Muſ. Lud. Ulr.* 414.
NOMADA.	Hiſtrio.	*Fab. Sp. Inſ.* 1.	
FORMICA.	Smaragdina.	N° 2.	
	Compreſſa	*Mantiſſ.* 2.	
	Cinerafcens.	12.	
	Elongata.	13.	
	Elevata.	*Sp. Inſ.* 26.	
	Bihamata.	29.	*Dr. Inſ.* 2. *t.* 38. *f.* 7. 8.
	Maxilloſa.	37.	
MUTILLA.	Indica.	*Lin. S. Nat.* 3.	*Muſ. Lud. Ulr.* 419.

ORDO IV. AGONATA.

CANCER.	Raninus. L.	*Fab. Sp. Inſ.* 1.	*Rumph. Muſ.* *t.* 7. *f.* T. V.
	Ceratopthalmus.	*Mant.* 6.	*Herbſt. Cancr.* 174. *t.* 1. *f.* 8. 9.
	Globus.	*Sp. Inſ.* 6.	
	Craniolaris. L.	7.	*Rumph. Muſ.* *t.* 10. *f.* A. B.
	Porcellanus.	*Mantiſſ.* 11.	*Herbſt. Cancr.* 92. 12. *t.* 2. *f.* 18.
	Corallinus.	23.	*Rumph. Muſ.* *t.* 8. *f.* 5.
	Floridus. L.	*Sp. Inſ.* 16.	*Herbſt. Cancr.* *t.* 3. *f.* 39.
	Vocans. L.	17.	*Petiv. Gaz.* *t.* 78. *f.* 5.
	Maculatus. L.	21.	*Rumph. Muſ.* *t.* 10. *f.* 1.
	Mænas. L.	25.	*t.* 6. *f.* O.
	Dormia. L.	27.	*t.* 11. *f.* 1.

	6-dentatus.	*Fab. Mantiss.*	Nº 43.	*Rumph. Amb.*	*t.* 1. *f.* 5.
	Feriatus L.	*Sp. Inf.*	28.	*Muf.*	*t.* 6. *f.* P.
	Pagurus. L.		29.		*t.* 11. *f.* 4.
	Æneus. L.		32.	*Seb. Muf.*	3. *t.* 19. *f.* 17.
	Fornicatus.	*Sp. Inf. App. p.*	502.		
	Ochtades.	*Mantiss.*	55.	*Herbst. Canc.*	*t.* 8. *f.* 54.
	Ovis.		66.		*f.* 74.
	Cylindrus.	*Sp. Inf.*	35.		
	Chabrus. L.		36.	*Muf. Lud. Ulr.*	438.
	Muricatus.	*Mantiss.*	67.	*Herbst. Cancr.*	*f.* 75.
	Erinaceus.		71.		
	Superciliofus. L.		72.	*Seb. Muf.*	3. *t.* 18. *f.* 11.
	Punctatus. L.	*Sp. Inf.*	44.	*Rumph. Amboin.*	*t.* 10. *f.* 6.
	7-fpinofus.	*Mant.*	75.		
	Horridus. L.	*Sp. Inf.*	51.	*Rumph. Muf.*	*t.* 9. *f.* 1.
	Longimanus L.		55.		*t.* 8. *f.* 2.
	Longipes. L.		56.		*t.* 8. *f.* 4.
	Spinifer. L.		57.	*Muf. Lud. Ulr.*	447.
PAGURUS.	Latro. L.		1.	*Rumph. Muf.*	*t.* 7. *f.* 4.
	Diogenes. L.		3.		*t.* 5. *f.* K. L.
	Hungarus.	*Mantiss.*	4.	*Herbf. Cancr.*	*t.* . *f.* 122.
	Miles.		6.		*f.* 114.
	Clypeatus.		7.		
HIPPA.	Adactyla ?	*Fab. Mantiss.*	Nº 1.		
	Dorfipes. L.		3.	*Rumph. Muf.*	*t.* 10. *f.* 3.
	Variolofa.		5.		
SCYLLARUS.	Arctus. L.	*Sp. Inf.*	1.		*t.* 2. *f.* 6. D;
ASTACUS.	Homarus. L.		3.		*t.* 1. *f.* A.

Emeritus.

	Emeritus. L. - - *Sp. Inf.* 16.	*Gron. Zooph.*	1000. *t.* 17. *f.* 8. 9.
SQUILLA.	Mantis. L. - - - - - - 1.	*Rumph. Muf.* - -	*t.* 3. *f.* 2.
	Scyllarus. L. - - - - - - 2.	*Seb. Muf.* - -	3. *t.* 20. *f.* 6.
	Ciliata. - - - - *Mantiff.* 3.		
	Chiragra ?- - - - *Sp. Inf.* 3.	*Rumph. Muf.* - -	*t.* 3. *f.* F.

ORDO V. UNOGATA.

LIBELLULA.	Indica. - - - *Fab. Sp. Inf.* 8.	*Drur. Inf.* - -	2. *t.* 46. *f.* 1.
	Fafciata. L. - - - - - - 17.	*Edw. Av.* - - -	*t.* 174.
	Americana. L. - - - - - 23.		
	Hiftrio. - - - *Mantiff.* 24.		
	Variegata. - *Lin. S. Nat.* 18.	*Amæn. Ac.* - -	6. *p.* 412. N° 86.
AGRION.	Ciliata. - - - *Fab. Sp. Inf.* 3.		
	Linearis. - - - - - - - 5.	*Drur. Inf.* - -	2. *t.* 48. *f.* 1.
JULUS.	Stigma. - - - - - - - 8.		
	Carnifex. - - - - - - - 9.	*Schroet. Abh.* -	1. *t.* 3. *f.* 7.
	Indus. L. - - - - - - 10.	*Petiv. Gaz.* -	*t.* 74. *f.* 3.
	Fufcus. L. - - - - - - 11.	*Seb. Muf.* - -	2. *t.* 24. *f.* 4. 5.
SCOLOPENDRA.	Morfitans. L. - - - - - 5.	*Petiv. Gaz.* - -	*t.* 13. *f.* 3.
	Dorfalis. - - - - - - - 7.		
	Clypeata. - - - - - - - 8.		
	Phofphorea. L. - - - - 11.		

Aranea.	Argentata.	*Fab. Sp. Inf.* 18.	
	Lusca.	51.	
Phalangium.	Caudatum. L.	7.	*Seb. Muf.* 1. *t.* 70. *f.* 7. 8.
Scorpio.	Afer. L.	3.	*Roef. Inf.* 3. *t.* 65.

ORDO VI. Glossata.

* Equites Troes.

Papilio.	Paris. L.	*Fab. Sp. Inf.* 2. N° 1.	*Drur. Inf.* 1. *t.* 12. *f.* 1.
	Theseus.	3.	*Cram. Inf.* 15. *t.* 180. B.
	Polytes. L.	4.	8. *t.* 90. B.
	Hector. L.	5.	12. *t.* 141. A.
	Romulus.		*t.* 43. A.
	Helenus. L.	7.	13. *t.* 153. A. B.
	Antenor.	8.	*Drur. Inf.* 2. *t.* 3. *f.* 1.
	Troilus. L.	9.	1. *t.* 11. *f.* 2. 3. 5?
	Palinurus.	*Fab. Mantiff.* N° 10.	
	Deiphobus. L.	*Sp. Inf.* 2. N° 10.	*Cram. Inf.* 16. *t.* 181. A. B.
	Pelaus.	12.	15. *t.* 177. A. B. C.
	Pammon. L.	16.	12. *t.* 141. B.
	Achates.	19.	16. *t.* 182. A. B.
	Polydorus. L.	20.	11. *t.* 128. A. B.
	Memnon. L. Var.	23.	*t.* 222. A. B.
	Priamus. L.	21.	2. *t.* 23. A. B.
	Remus.	22.	1. *t.* 10. A. B. & 11. A. B.
	Agenor. L.	25.	3. *t.* 32. A. B.
	Amphrisius.	*Mantiff.* 23.	19. *t.* 219. A.

Alcandor.

Alcandor.				*t.*40.A.B.D.E.
Sarpedon. L.	*Spec. Inſ.*	28.		11.*t.* 122. D. E.
Amphimedon.		31.		17.*t.* 194. A.'
Æneas. L.		32.		3.*t.* 29. C.—F.
Lyſander.		33.		2.*t.* 24. E.?
Polymneſtor.		35.		5.*t.* 53. A. B.
Panthous. L.		36.		11.*t.* 123. 124.
Remus.	*Mantiſſ.*	24.		12.*t.*135.A.136.A.
Pandarus. L.	*Spec.*	37.	*Muſ. Lud. Ulr.*	198.
Aſtenous.		38.	*Cram. Inſ.*	17.*t.* 195. A.

** Equites Achivi.

Ripheus.	*Fab. Mantiſſ.* N°	43.	*Cram. Inſ.*	*t.* 385. A. B.
Pyrrhus. L.	*Sp. Inſ.* 2. N°	41.		*t.* 220. A. B.
Tiridates.		43.		*t.* 161. A. B.
Aeclus.	*Mantiſſ.*	50.		*t.* 317. A. B.
Fabius.	*Sp. Inſ.* N°	47.		
Cocles.	*Mantiſſ.*	53.		
Leilus. L.	*Sp. Inſ.*	48.		*t.* 85. C. D.
Ulyſſes. L.		52.		*t.* 121. A. B.
Patroclus. L.		53.		*t.* 109. A. B.
Diomedes. L.		54.		*t.* 122. A.
Varanes.		55.		*t.* 160. D. E.
Alcibiades.	*Mantiſſ.*	65.		
Pompilius.		66.		*t.* 37. A. B.
Sinon.	*Sp. Inſ.*	59.	*Drur. Inſ.*	*t.* 22. *f.* 3. 4.
Antheus			*Cram. Inſ.*	*t.* 235. B. C.
Chiron.		60.		*t.* 200. D. E.
Curius.	*Mantiſſ.*	71.		
Periander.		74.		
Codrus.	*Sp. Inſ.*	69.		*t.* 179. A. B.
Meneſtheus.		74.		*t.* 142. A. B.
Xuthus. L.		75.		*t.* 73. A. B.

Cresphontes.	*Sp. Inf.* 77.	*Cram. Inf.*	*t.* 89. A. B.
Orontes. L.	80.		*t.* 83. A. B.
Ægiſtus.			*t.* 241. C. D.
Agamemnon. L.	81.		*t.* 106. C. D.
Ægiſtheus. L.	N° 82.		*t.* 200. A. B. C.
Empedocles.	*Mantiſſ.* 94.		
Euryalus.	*Sp. Inſ.* 83.		*t.* 74. A. B.
Phidippus. L.	85.		*t.* 69. A. B.
Niſus.	84.		*t.* 150. A. B.
Aurelius.	86.		*t.* 168. A. B.
Demoleus. L.	87.		*t.* 231. A. B.
Medon. L.	89.		*t.* 205. B. C.
Philoctetes. L.	90.		*t.* 20. A. B. C.
Nireus. L.	93.		*t.* 187. A. B.
Amphimachus.	94.		*t.* 84. A. B.?
Amphitrion.	96.		*t.* 157. A. B.
Gambriſius.	*Fab. Mantiſſ.* 113.		*t.* 43. F. G.
Druſius.			*t.* 229. A. 230. A
Demophon. L.	*Sp. Inſ.* 97.		*t.* 158. A.—E.
Eurypylus. L.	106.		*t.* 122. B. C.
Aſtenous.			*t.* 208. A. B.
Sabinus.	*Sp. Inſ. Ap. p.* 502.		*t.* 289. A.—D.
Jaſon.	*Lin. S. Nat.* N° 38.	*Muſ. Lud. Ulr.* 210.	

*** Heliconii.

Calliope. L.	*Fab. Sp. Inſ.* 107.	*Cram. Inſ.*	*t.* 246. C.
Melite. L.	108.		*t.* 153. C. D.
Mopſa. L.	109.		*t.* 190. D.
Mneme. L.	110.		*t.* 190. C.
Lybia.	111.		*t.* 177. C. D.
Violæ. L.	112.		*t.* 298. D. E.
Terpſichore. L.	113.		*t.* 298. A. B. C.
Serena.	114.		*t.* 268. A. B.

Urania.

Urania. L.	*Fab. Sp. Inſ.* N°	117.	*Muſ. Lud. Ulr.*	225.
Pſidii. L.		124.	*Cram. Inſ.*	*t.* 257. P.
Aſpaſia.	*Mantiſſ.*	145.		
Ægle.	*Sp. Inſ.*	125.		*t.* 126. C. D. ?
Thalia. L.		130.		*t.* 246. A.
Euryta. L.		131.		*t.* 233. A. B.
Aedea. L.		132.	*Clerck. Ic.*	*t.* 41. *f.* 2.
Antiocha. L.		134.	*Cram. Inſ.*	*t.* 38. E. F.
Erato. L.		146.		*t.* 119. A.
Aſſarica.				*t.* 363. A. B.

**** Parnassii.

Quirina.	152.		
Piera. L.	153.		*t.* 291. C. D.
Paſithoe. L.	154.		*t.* 258. E. F.
Andromeda.	158.		
Idea. L.	160.		*t.* 193. A. B.

***** Danai Candidi.

Braſſicæ. L.	161.		*t.* 271. E. F.
Napi. L.	163.	*Albin. Inſ.*	*t.* 52. F. G.
Valeria.		*Cram. Inſ.*	*t.* 85. A.
Libythea.	172.		
Creona.	175.		*t.* 95. C.—F.
Neriſſa.			*t.* 44. A.
Demophile. L.	177.	*Clerck. Ic.*	*t.* 28. *f.* 4.
Crocale.		*Cram. Inſ.*	*t.* 55. C. D.
Hecabe. L.	178.		*t.* 124. B. C.
Druſilla.			*t.* 110. C.
Paulina.			*t.* 110. E. F.
Xiphia.	180.		
Hedyle.			*t.* 186. C. D.

Eucharis. - *Fab. Sp. Inf.* N° 181. *Cram. Inf.* - - - *t.* 352. C.D.E.F.
Jugurtha. - - - - - - - - - *t.* 187. E. F.
Alcmeone. - - - - - - 186. - - - - - - *t.* 141. E.
Oenippe. - - - - - - - - - *t.* 229. B. C.
Pyranthe. L. - - - - - 188. *Muf. Lud. Ulr.* 245.
Catilla. - - - - - - - - - *t.* 229. E. F.
Leucippe. - - - - - - 189. *Cram. Inf.* - - - *t.* 36. A.—C.
Thetis. - - - - - - - - - *t.* 238. F. G.
Callirhoe. - - - - - - 190. *Pl. Enlum.* - - *t.* 91. *f.* 1. 2.
Mefentina. - - - - - - - - - *t.* 270. A. B.
Glaucippe. L. - - - - - 191. *Cram. Inf.* - - - *t.* 164. A.—C.
Zelmira. - - - - - - - - - *t.* 320. C.—F.
Euippe. L. - - - - - - 192. - - - - - - *t.* 91. D.—G.?
Coronnis. - - - - - - 193. - - - - - - *t.* 44. B. C.
Hyparete. L. - - - - - 194. *Clerck. Ic.* - - - *t.* 38. *f.* 2. 3.
Evagete. - - - - - - - - *Cram. Inf.* - - - *t.* 221. F. G.
Scylla. L. - - - - - - 203. - - - - - - *t.* 12. C. D.
Coronea. - - - - - - 201. - - - - - - *t.* 68. B. C.
Cornelia. - - - *Mantiff.* 229.
Agathina. - - - - - - - - - *t.* 237. D. E.
Judith. - - - - - - - 230.
Belifamæ. - - - - - - - - - *t.* 258. A.B.C.D
Amata. - - - *Sp. Inf.* 204.
Ænippe. - - - - - - - - - *t.* 157. C. D.
Cypræa. - - - *Mantiff.* 232.
Hilaria. - - - - - - - - - *t.* 339. E. F.
Danaë. - - - *Sp. Inf.* 205.
Sefia. - - - - *Mantiff.* 234. - - - - - - *t.* 217. C.D.E.
Rahel. - - - - - - - 235.
Ada. - - - - - - - - - *t.* 363. C. D.
Meffalina. - - - - - - 236.
Zeuxippe. - - - - - - - - - *t.* 362. E. F.
Gnoma. - - - *Sp. Inf.* 217. - - - - - - *t.* 361. C. D.
Drya. - - - - - - - 218. - - - - - - *t.* 120. C. D.
Philea. L. - - - - - - 221. - - - - - - *t.* 173. E. F.
Dorimenes. - - - - - - - - - *t.* 387. C. D.

Acafta.

Acaſta.	*Lin. S. Nat.* N°	83.	*Muſ. Lud. Ulr.*	250.
Encedonia.		90.		244.
Arſalte.		91.	*Clerck. Ic.*	*t.* 23. *f.* 2.
Damone.		93.		

† Danai Festivi.

Midamus. L.	*Fab. Sp. Inſ.*	227.	*Cram. Inſ.*	*t.* 266. A. B.
Claudius.	*Mantiſſ.*	261.		*t.* 266. C.
Climene.				*t.* 389. E. F.
Liberius.	*Sp. Inſ.*	229.		*t.* 210. G. H.
Syphax.		234.		*t.* 233. C. D.
Eyialeus.	*Mantiſſ.*	267.		*t.* 189. D. E.
Eualthe.	*Sp. Inſ.*	235.		*t.* 17. E. F.
Cæneus. L.		239.	*Muſ. Lud. Ulr.*	271.
Genutia.			*Cram. Inſ.*	*t.* 206. C. D.
Pinthæus. L.		242.		*t.* 258.
Chryſippus. L.		245.		*t.* 118. B. C.
Hegeſippus.		248.		*t.* 180. A.
Nicaeus.		251.		*t.* 12. G. H.
Gripus.		255.		*t.* 183. C. D.
Xanthus. L.		257.		*t.* 183. A. B.
Arceſilaus.	*Mantiſſ.*	305.		
Eribotes.	*Sp. Inſ.*	267.		
Morvus.		270.		*t.* 48. A. B.
Cocytus.	*Mantiſſ.*	316.		
Obrinus. L.	*Sp. Inſ.*	275.		*t.* 338. C. D.
Ancæus. L.		276.		*t.* 49. E. F.
Jairus.		281.		*t.* 6. A. B.
Philocles. L.		285.		*t.* 184. D. E. F.
Aeropus. L.		287.		*t.* 111. F. G.
Mineus.		294.		*t.* 84. C. D.
Baldus.		306.		
Zetes.	*Lin. S. Nat.* N°	110.	*Clerck. Ic.*	*t.* 43. *f.* 1.
Enceladus.		112.	*Muſ. Lud. Ulr.*	254.

Eribote.	- *Lin. S. Nat.* N° 115.	*Muf. Lud. Ulr.*		233.
Perius.	- - - - - - - 116.	- - - - -		261.
Philomelus.	- - - - - 123.	*Amœn. Ac.*	- -	6. *p.* 404. 60.

* NYMPHALES GEMMATI.

Polynice.	- *Fab. Sp. Inf.* N° 310.	*Cram. Inf.* - - -	*t.* 195. D. E.
Almana. L.	- - - - - 311.	- - - - - -	*t.* 58. F. G.
Afterie. L.	- - - - - - 312.	- - - - - -	*t.* 58. D. E.
Oenone. L.	- - - - - 313.	- - - - - -	*t.* 35. A. C.
Erigone.	- - - - - - - -	- - - - - -	*t.* 62. E. F.
Lemonias. L.	- - - - - 314.	- - - - - -	*t.* 35. D. F.
Villida.	- - - *Mantiff.* 366.		
Glycerie.	- - - - - - 379.		
Orithya. L.	- - *Sp. Inf.* 315.	- - - - - -	*t.* 32. E. F.
Remulia.	- - - - - - - -	- - - - - -	*t.* 232. F. G.
Feronia. L.	- - - - - 318.	- - - - - -	*t.* 192. E. F.
Lampetia. L.	- *Mantiff.* 378.	- - - - - -	*t.* 148. D. D. *t.* 349. A. B.
Roxelana.	- - - *Sp. Inf.* 320.	- - - - - -	*t.* 141. C. D.
Minerva.	- - - - - - 327.	- - - - - -	*t.* 116. E. F.
Laomedia. L.	- - - - - 333.	- - - - - -	*t.* 8. F. G.
Cardui.	- - - - - - - 364.	- - - - - -	*t.* 26. E. F.
Atlita.	- - - - *Mant.* 388.		
Libye. L.	- - - *Sp. Inf.* 334.	*Sultz. Inf.* - - -	*t.* 17. *f.* 7.
Juftina.	- - - - - - - - -	- *Cram. Inf.* - -	*t.* 326. C.
Hedonia. L.	- - - - - 335.	- - - - - -	*t.* 69. C. D.
Arfinoë. L.	- - - - - 343.	- - - - - -	*t.* 160. B. C.
Panthera.	- - *Mantiff.* 407.	-	
Pipleis. L.	- - *Sp. Inf.* 368.	- - - - - -	*t.* 60. A. B.
Claudia.	- - - - - - 369.	*Naturforch.* 9. - -	*t.* 2.
Bankia.	- - - - - - - 371.	*Cram. Inf.* - - -	*t.* 26. A. B. & 291. I.
Leda.	- - - - - - - 376.	- - - - - -	*t.* 196. C. D.
Rohria.	- - - *Mantiff.* 446.		

Arcenfia.

Arcensia.			Cram. Inf.	t. 292. D. E.
Constantia.				t. 133. A. B.
Polydecta.	Fab. Sp. Inf. N°	373.		t. 144. E. F.
Iphita.		379.		t. 209. C. D.
Tolumnia.		374.		t. 130. F. G.
Erminia.				t. 176. A. B.
Morna.		375.		
Polibete.				t. 234. D. E. & 235. C. D.
Juliana.	Fab. Sp. Inf. App. p. 503.			t. 280. A. B.
Egista.				t. 281. C. D.
Helie.	Lin. S. Nat. N°	152.	Clerck. Ic.	t. 34. f. 3.
Arete.			Cram. Inf.	t. 313. E. F.

** Nymphales Phalerati.

Ida.			Cram. Inf.	t. 42. C. D. & 374. C. D.
Cydippe. L.	Fab. Sp. Inf.	388.		t. 62. A. B.
Penthesilia.		390.		t. 145. B. C.
Melita.				t. 28. D. E.
Cyane.		392.	Drur. Inf.	1. t. 4. f. 1.
Vitellia.	Mantiss.	474.	Cram. Inf.	t. 349. E. F.
Antilope.				t. 18[illegible]. E. F.
Protogenia.	Sp. Inf.	395.		t. 189. F. G.
Atalanta.		397.		t. 84. E. F. Var.
Charonia.		398.		t. 47. A. B. C.
Polychloros. L.		404.		t. 330. C. D. Var.
Juventa.				t. 188. B.
Dirce. L.		407.		t. 212. C. D.
Hippoclus.				t. 222. C. D.
C. Aureum. L.		410.		t. 19. E. F.
Ariadne. L.		412.		t. 144. G. H.
Proserpina.				t. 218. C. D.
Bolinæ. L.		414.		t. 65. E. F.

Lisionassæ. - - - - - - - *Cram. Inʃ.* - - *t.* 205. A. B.
Clytia. L. - - - *Sp. Inʃ.* 415. *Muʃ. Lud. Ulr.* 296.
Thyonneus. - - - - - - - *Cram. Inʃ.* - - - - *t.* 222. E. F.
Archesia. - - *Sp. App. p.* 504. - - - - - - *t.* 219. D. E.
Amathea. L. - *Spec. Inʃ.* N° 416. - - - - - - *t.* 209. A. B.
Undularis. - *Sp. App. p.* 504. - - - - - - *t.* 256. A. B.
Monina. - - *Mantiʃʃ.* N° 502.
Lamis. - - - - - - - - - - - - - - - - - *t.* 238. E.
Allica. - - - - - - N° 510. - - - - - - *t.* 280. E. F.
Leucothoë L. - *Sp. Inʃ.* 421. - - - - - - *t.* 203. E. F.?
Melicerta. - - - - - - 423. - - - - - - *t.* 212. E. F.
Heliodore. - - *Mantiʃʃ.* 516.
Ilithuia. - - - *Sp. Inʃ.* 426. - - - - - - *t.* 213. A. B.
Pelea. - - - *Mantiʃʃ.* 523.
Erymanthis. - - - - - - - - - - - - - - - *t.* 238. F. G.
Venilia. L. - - *Sp. Inʃ.* 431. - - - - - - *t.* 219. B. C.
Alimena. L. - - - 432. - - - - - - *t.* 221. A. B. C.
Phœrusa. L. - - - - - 433. - - - - - - *t.* 130. B. C.
Manilia. - - - - - - - - - - - - - - - - *t.* 259. A. B.
Hippona. - - - - - - 434. - - - - - - *t.* 90. C. D.
Adonia. - - - - - - - - - - - - - - - - *t.* 259. C. D.
Agatha. - - - *Mantiʃʃ.* 530.
Neærea. L. - - *Sp. Inʃ.* 441. - - - - - - *t.* 75. C. D.
Aceste. L. - - - - - - 442. - - - - - - *t.* 121. E. F.
Porphyria. - - - - - - - - - - - - - - - *t.* 259. E. F.
Eurinome. - - - - - - 443. - - - - - - *t.* 70. A.
Neste. - - - - - - - - - - - - - - - - - *t.* 256. E. F.
Dissimilis. L. - - - - - 444. - - - - - - *t.* 82. C. D.
Assimilis. L. - - - - - 445. - - - - - - *t.* 154. A.
Similis. L. - - - - - - 446. - - - - - - *t.* 30. D.
Lotis. - - - - - - - - - - - - - - - - - *t.* 230. D. E.
Lais. - - - - - - - - 448. - - - - - - *t.* 110. A. B.
Valentina. - - - - - - - - - - - - - - - *t.* 327. C. D.
Egialea. - - - - - - 449. - - - - - - *t.* 192. D.
Alcippe. - - - - - - - - - - - - - - - - *t.* 389. G. H.
Panope. - - - - - - 450. - - - - - - *t.* 65. C. D.

Villida,

Villida. - - - - - - - - - *Cram. Inf.* - - - *t.* 349. C. D.
Hippia. - - - *Mantiff.* 545.
Martha. - - - - - - - 555.
Elea. - - - - - *Sp. Inf.* 460. - - - - - - *t.* 242. D. E.
Cytherea. L. - - - - - 474. *Clerck. Ic.* - - - *t.* 39. *f.* 3.
Phalantha. *Fab. Sp. Inf.* N° 485. *Drur. Inf.* - - 1. *t.* 21. *f.* 1. 2.
Tipha. - *Lin. S. Nat.* N° 164. *Clerck. Ic.* - - - *t.* 32. *f.* 3.
Canace. - - - - - - - 173. *Drur. Inf.* - - 1. *t.* 15. *f.* 1. 2.
Idmone. - - - - - - 182. *Muf. Lud. Ulr.* 310.
Elea. - - - - - - 183. *Drur. Inf.* - - 2. *t.* 17. *f.* 5. 6.
Janaffa. - - - - - - - 185. *Muf. Lud. Ulr.* 294.
Nauplia. - - - - - - 197. *Clerck. Ic.* - - - *t.* 46. *f.* 1. 2.
Hypermneftra. - - - - - 198. *Amœn. Ac.* - - 6. *p.* 407. 69.
Nefæa. - - - - - - - 199. *Muf. Lud. Ulr.* 302.

† Plebeii Rurales.

Amor. - - *Fab. Sp. Inf.* 491.
Vulcanus. - - - - - - - *Cram. Inf.* - - - *t.* 208. E. F.
Lifias. - - - *Mantiff.* 615.
Etolus. - - - - - - - 620.
Ganymedes. - - *Sp. Inf.* 500. - - - - - - - *t.* 40. C. D.
Sphinx. - - - - - - - 511. - - - - - - - *t.* 46. F. G.
Hyacinthus. - - - - - 516. - - - - - - - *t.* 36. C. D.
Iarbus. - - - *Mantiff.* 648.
Bæticus. L. - - *Sp. Inf.* 529. *Ernft. Pap. d' Eur.* *t.* 37. *f.* 76.
Strephon. - - - - - - 531.
Atymnus. - - *Mantiff.* 662. *Cram. Inf.* - - - *t.* 331. D. E.
Aeolus. - - - *Sp. Inf.* 535. *Pl. Enlum.* - - *t.* 18. *f.* 6. 7.
Simæthis. - - - - - - 537. *Drur. Inf.* - - 1. *t.* 1. *f.* 3.
Ixion. - - - - - - - 540.
Nedymond. - - - - - - - *Cram. Inf.* - - - *t.* 299. E. F.
Rofimon. - - - - - - 541.
Laius. - - - - - - - - - - - - - - - - *t.* 319. D. E.
Amyntor. - - - - - - 543. - - - - - - - *t.* 159. D. E.

Triopas.

Triopas. - - - - - - - - *Cram. Inf.* - - - t. 310. G. H.
Eumolphus. - - - - - - - - - - - - - - t. 299. G. H.
Hylax. - - *Fab. Sp. Inf.* 559.
Midas. - - - - - - - 564.
Melampus. - - - - - - - - - - - - - - t. 362. G. H.
Æsopus. - - - - - - 565. *Drur. Inf.* - - 2. t. 9. f. 3. 4.
Phædrus. - - - - - - 566. *Cram. Inf.* - - - t. 238. C.
Aratus. - - - - - - - - - - - - - - - t. 365. A. B.
Cephus. - - - - - - - 576.
Petavius. - - - - - - - - - - - - - - t. 365. C. D.
Haraldus. - - *Mantiss.* 744.
Ubaldus. - - - - - - - - - - - - - - - t. 390. L. M.
Neleus. L. - - *Sp. Inf.* 581. *Clerck. Ic.* - - - t. 45. f. 2.
Bochus. - - - - - - - - *Cram. Inf.* - - - t. 391. C. D.
Priassus. L. - - - - - - 591. *Mus. Lud. Ulr.* 319.
Polybe. - *Lin. S. Nat.* N° 218. *Amæn. Ac.* - - 6. p. 404. 58.
Timantes. - - - - - - 241. *Mus. Lud. Ulr.* 322.
Peleus. - - - - - - - 249. *Clerck. Ic.* - - - t. 45. f. 5.

†† PLEBEII URBICOLÆ.

Exclamationis. *Fab. Sp. Inf.* N° 595.
Augias. L. - - - - - - 597. *Amæn. Ac.* - - 6. p. 410. 80.
Colon. - - - - - - - - 598.
Alcithoë. - - - - - - - - *Cram. Inf.* - - - t. 80. C. D.
Alexis. - - - - - - - 619.
Thrax. L. - - - - - - 620. - - - - - - - 6. t. 68. E.
Dan. - - - - *Mantiss.* 798.
Chromus. - - - - - - - - - - - - - - t. 284. E.
Ladon. - - - - - - - - - - - - - - - t. 284. G.
Gnetus. - *Fab. Sp. Inf.* N° 624. *Pl. Enl.* - - - t. 18. f. 8. 9.
Polycletus. L. - - - - - 627. *Cram. Inf.* - - - t. 159. F. G.
Coridon. - - - - - - - - - - - - - - - t. 340. C. D. E.
Phidias. L. - - - - - 632. - - - - - - - t. 41. C. D.
Japetus. - - - - - - - - - - - - - - - t. 365. E. F.

Maimon.

Maimon. - *Fab. Sp. Inf.* N° 635. *Cram. Inf.* - - - *t.* 22. C. ?
Foreftan. - - - - - - - - - - - - - - - *t.* 391. E. F.
Menalcas. - - - - - - 639.
Celænus. - - - - - - - - - - - - - - - *t.* 393. A. B.
Spio. L. - - - - - - 645. *Muf. Lud. Ulr.* 330.
Menes. - - - - - - - - - - - - - - - *t.* 393. H. I.
Pygmæus. - - - - - - 646.
Butes. - *Lin. S. Nat.* N° 261. *Clerck. Ic.* - - - *t.* 46. *f.* 6.
Phaleros. - - - - - - 272.
Cereus. - - - - - - 273.

SPHINX. Afiliformis. - *Fab. Sp. Inf.* N° 6.
Nerii. - - - - - - - 11. *Cram. Inf.* - - - *t.* 224. D.
Hypothoüs. - - - - - - - - - - - - - *t.* 285. D.
Dentata. - - - - - - - 16. - - - - - - *t.* 125. G.
Ancæus. - - - - - - - - - - - - - - *t.* 355. A.
Alope. - - - - - *Mantiff.* 19. - - - - - - *t.* 301. G.
Opheltes. - - - - - - - - - - - - - - *t.* 285. B.
Ello. L. - - - *Sp. Inf.* 17. *Drur. Inf.* - - 1. *t.* 27. *f.* 3.
Acteus. - - - - - - - - - *Cram. Inf.* - - - *t.* 248. A.
Atropos. L. - - - - - - 23. - - - - - - *t.* 78. A. & 237. A.
Phorbas. - - - - - - - 25. - - - - - - *t.* 55. B.
Chiron. - - - - - - - - - - - - - - - *t.* 137. E.
Pagana. - - - - - - - 29.
Oldenlandiæ. - - - - - 37.
Phalaris. - - - - - - - - - - - - - - - *t.* 149. A.
Lycetus. - - - - - - 38. - - - - - - *t.* 61. D.
Panopus. - - - - - - - - - - - - - - *t.* 222. A. B.
Boerhaaviæ. - - - - - - 39. *Sultz. Inf.* - - - *t.* 20. *f.* 3.
Efon. - - - - - - - - - *Cram. Inf.* - - - *t.* 226. C.
Minus. - - - *Mantiff.* 44.
Drancus. - - - - - - - - - - - - - - - *t.* 132. F.
Porcellus. L. - - - *Sp. Inf.* 44. *Ernft. Pap.* - - *t.* 112. N° 161.
Convolvuli. L. - - - - - 46. *Cram. Inf.* - - - *t.* 225. D.

	Celerio. L.	*Sp. Inf.* 50. *Cram. Inf.*	*t.* 125. E.
	Neſſus.		*t.* 226. D.
	Crantor	*Fab. Sp. Inf.* N° 51.	*t.* 104. A.
	Alecto. L.	52.	*t.* 137. D.
	Gnoma.	53.	*t.* 152. A.
	Menephron.		*t.* 285. A.
	Heſpera.	54.	
	Faro.		*t.* 285. C.
	Butus.	*Mantiſſ.* 62.	
	Vampyrus.	66.	
	Ocypete?	*Lin. S. Nat.* N° 4. *Muſ. Lud. Ulr.* 344.	
	Megæra.	21. *Clerck. Ic.*	*t.* 47. *f.* 2.
	Tiſiphone.	23. *Muſ. Lud. Ulr.* 359.	
	Brennus.	*Cram. Inf.*	*t.* 398. B.
Sesia.	Ixion. L.	*Fab. Sp. Inf.* N° 2.	*t.* 68. F.
	Octomaculata.	8.	
	Hippotes.		*t.* 286. A.
	Hæmorrhoidalis.	13.	*t.* 52. C. D.?
	Feneſtrata.	15.	*t.* 251. D.
Zygæna.	Grus.		*t.* 368. A.
	Diptera.	44.	
	Aurata.		*t.* 264. A.
	Creuſa.	*Lin. S. Nat.* N° 39. *Clerck. Ic.*	*t.* 46. *f.* 3.?
	Cyſſeus.	*Cram. Inf.*	*t.* 355. B.
	Atereus.		*t.* 400. A.
	Bombyliformis.		*t.* 400. C.
Bombyx.	Paphia. L.	*Fab. Sp. Inf.* N° 4.	*t.* 147. A. B.
	Laocoon.		*t.* 117. A. B. C.
	Mylitta.	7.	*t.* 146. A.
	Fabia.		*t.* 250. B.

Luna. L.	*Fab. Sp. Ins.* 15.	*Cram. Ins.*	*t.* 31. A. B.
Fenestra. L.	18.	*Clerck. Ic.*	*t.* 55. *f.* 1.
Polybia.		*Cram. Ins.*	*t.* 369. A.
Penelope.	19.		*t.* 45. A.
Jana.			*t.* 396. A.
Perspicua. L.	21.	*Mus. Lud. Ulr.* 373.	
Conspicillator.		*Cram. Ins.*	*t.* 97. A. B.
Militaris. L.	22.		*t.* 29. B.
Numana.			*t.* 227. A. 228. A.
Eugenia.			*t.* 398. M.
Promula.	34.		*t.* 72. D.
Aconyta.			*t.* 131. A.
Quadricincta.	*Mantiss.* 44.		
Barbara.			*t.* 368. B.
Lusca.	49.		
Niceta.			*t.* 368. C.
Hibisci.	*Sp. Ins.* 45.		
Glauca.			*t.* 368. D.
Imperialis.	62.	*Drur. Ins.*	1. *t.* 9. *f.* 1.
Lunata.		*Cram. Ins.*	*t.* 369. C.
Crassicornis.	63.		
Silvandra.			*t.* 369. D.
Pasinuntia.			*t.* 367. H.
Nuda.	*Mantiss.* 105.		
Evergista.			*t.* 369. E.
Hyphinoe.			*t.* 154. B.
Flava.	*Sp. Ins.* 82.		
Petosiris.			*t.* 397. D.
Rutila.	*Mantiss.* 131.		
Chrysorrhea.	*Spec. Ins.* 102.	*Roes. Ins.*	1. *ph.* 2. *t.* 22.
Nitidula.	*Mantiss.* 153.		
Cyane.	*Sp. App. p.* 506.	*Cram. Ins.*	*t.* 267. D.
Crotalariæ.	*Sp. Ins.* 126.		1. *t.* 5. C. D.
Ricini.	127.		
Lectrix.	132.		*t.* 192. C.
Sanguinolenta.	128.		*t.* 183. D.

	Lepida.	*Cram. Inſ.*	*t.* 130. E.
	Franciſca.	*Mantiſſ.* 200.	
	Monycha.		*t.* 131. C.
	Jeſuita.	*Sp. Inſ.* 145.	
	Lactinia.		*t.* 133. D.
	Glorioſæ.	150.	
	Brotea.		*t.* 322. E.
	Crini.	151.	
	Punctigera.	*Lin. S. Nat.* 151. *Clerck. Ic.*	*t.* 50. *f.* 3.
NOCTUA.	Strix. L.	*Fab. Sp. Inſ.* 3. *Cram. Inſ.*	*t.* 145. A.
	Ulula.	9.	*t.* 174. E.
	Materna. L.	16.	*t.* 174. A. B.
	Itynx.	*Mantiſſ.* 10.	
	Mineus.		*t.* 131. D.
	Crepuſcularis. L.	*Fab. Sp. Inſ.* 11.	*t.* 159. A.
	Irrorata.	*Fab. Sp. App. p.* 506.	
	Lyncea.	506.	
	Sinuata.	507.	
	Squalida.	*Fab. Mant.* N° 13.	
	Veſpertilio.	16.	
	Retorta.		*t.* 116. D.
	Illibata.	*Sp. Inſ.* 13.	
	Obſcura.		*t.* 274. B.
	Umminia.	*Sp. App. p.* 506.	*t.* 267. F.
	Inara.		*t.* 239. E.
	Scrobiculata.	*Sp. Inſ.* N° 14.	
	Carenea.		*t.* 269. E. F.
	Dioſcoreæ.	15.	*t.* 30. A.—C.
	Materna.	16.	*t.* 174. A. B.
	Hypermneſtra.		*t.* 323. A. B.
	Cephiſe.		*t.* 227. B.
	Paphos.	*Mantiſſ.* 24.	
	Chione.	*Sp. Inſ.* 26.	
	Saga.	*Mantiſſ.* 29.	

Bajularia.

Bajularia.	*Sp. Inf.*	23.	*Cram. Inf.*	*t.* 172. C.
Aſtrea.		21.		
Convoluta.		30.		*t.* 208. D.
Membliaria.				*t.* 269. C. D.
Ficus.		33.		
Luſca.	*Mantiſſ.*	49.		
Manlia.		36.		*t.* 92. A.
Caricæ.		34.		*t.* 133. E. 242. A. B.
Leonina.		38.		
Fulvia. L.		43.	*Clerck. Ic.*	*t.* 55. *f.* 6.
Avida.	*Fab. Mantiſſ.*	68.		
Triangulum.		74.		
Arcuata.		75.		
Vulpina.	*Sp. Inf.*	50.		
Tigrina.		52.		
Mezentina.			*Cram. Inf.*	*t.* 323. F.
Cyllaria.				*t.* 251. C. D.
Geometrica.		53.		
Stolida.		54.		
Undata.		60.		
Ammonia.				*t.* 250. D.
Vittata.		N° 61.		
Hyppaſia.				*t.* 250. E.
Frugalis.		62.		
Flava.		63.		
Stigmatizans.		64.		
Alphea.				*t.* 250. F.
Equeſtris.		65.		
Javana.				*t.* 274. C.
Dorſalis.	*Mantiſſ.*	103.		
Luminoſa.				*t.* 274. D.
Rejecta.	*Sp. Inf.*	66.		
Achatina.				*t.* 273. E. 288. A.
Elata.		67.		
Archeſia.				*t.* 273. F. G.

	Mercatoria.	79. *Cram. Inf.*	*t.* 62. C. D.
	Timais.		*t.* 275. B.
	Rapta.	*Mantiff.* 120.	
	Orofia.		*t.* 275. D.
	Partita.	*Sp. Inf.* 80.	
	Melanthus.		*t.* 286. B.
	Pagana.	90.	
	Joviana.		*t.* 399. B.
	Orichalcea.	92.	
	Clytia.		*t.* 399. G.
	Signata.	96.	
	Dominica.		*t.* 399. H.
	Peponis.	97.	
	Nitidula.	*Mantiff.* 153.	
	Sinuata.	*Sp. Inf.* 116.	
	Amphix.		*t.* 134. C.
	Hiftrionica.	117.	
	Perithea.		*t.* 172. D.
	Pellex.	*Lin. S. Nat.* N° 104. *Muf. Lud. Ulr.* 388.	
	Interrupta.	116. *Cram. Inf.*	*t.* 185.
PHALÆNA.	Strigaria.	*Fab. Sp. Inf.* N° 12.	*t.* 133. C.
	Undaria.	20.	
	Monilaria.	23.	
	Rondelaria.	24.	
	Macularia.	27.	*t.* 129. C.
	Ocularia.	38.	
	Perdica.		*t.* 178. F.
	Hefperia.		*t.* 251. B.
	Flavaria.	*Fab. Mant.* N° 32.	
	Margaritaria.		*t.* 367. K.
	Tripunctaria. L.	*Sp. Inf.* 47.	*t.* 22. E.
	Caudata.	64.	*t.* 104. D.
	Lateraria.	*Mantiff.* 77.	
	Lactucina.		*t.* 273. B. C.

Venaria.

Venaria. - - - *Sp. Inf.* 52. *Cram. Inf.* - - - *t.* 29. A.
Zemire. - - - - - - - - - - - - *t.* 367. I.
Obliquaria. - - *Mantiff.* 81.
Rofalia. - - - - - - - - - - - - *t.* 368. F.
Erneftina. - - - - - - - - - - - - *t.* 369. F.
Sangarida. - - - - - - - - - - - - *t.* 381. D.
Caudata. - - - *Sp. Inf.* 64. - - - - - *t.* 104. D.
Fafciata. - - - - - - - 65.
Vulpenaria. - - - - - - - - - - - - *t.* 400. O. P.
Arcuata. - - - *Mantiff.* 104.
Pamphilia. - - - - - - - - - - - - *t.* 368. G.
Liturata. - - - - - - 109.
Coleta. - - - - - - - - - - - - *t.* 368. H.
Irrorata. - - - *Sp. Inf.* 77.
Carinenta. - - - - - - 78. - - - - - - *t.* 128. F.
Eufebia. - - - - - - - - - - - - *t.* 369. G. H.
Flaveolata. - - - - - - 91. - - - - - - *t.* 88. C.
Fimbriata. - - - - - - - - - - - - *t.* 398. O.
Janata. L. - - - - - - 121. *Muf. Lud. Ulr.* 398.
Expectata. - - - - - - 123.
Cribrata. - - - - - - 133. *Cram. Inf.* - - - *t.* 208. C. G.
Marginata. - - - - - - - - - - - - *t.* 400. I.
Æftuata. L. - - - - - 149. *Muf. Lud. Ulr.* 397.
Capitata. - - - - - - 148.
Sulphurata. - - - - - 152.
Flavata. - - - - - - - - - - - - *t.* 307. C.
Violata. - - - *Mantiff.* 238.
Securata. - - - - - - 242.
Canenta. - - - - - - - - - - - - *t.* 250. C.
Perfpectata. - - *Sp. Inf.* 163.
Vitrata. - - - *Mantiff.* 255.
Revidata. - - - - - - 258.
Derogata. - - - *Sp. Inf.* 166.
Ejectata. - - - - - - 167.
Sagittalis. - *Fab. Sp. Inf.* 179.
Amando. - - - - - - - - *Cram. Inf.* - - *t.* 247. E.

Fufcalis.

	Fuscalis. - *Fab. Sp. Inf.* 182.			
	Pueritia. - - - - - - - -	*Cram. Inf.* - - -		*t.* 264. E.
	Angustalis. - - *Mantiss.* 309.			
	Procopia. - - - - - - - - - - - - - -			*t.* 368. E.
	Recurvalis. - - *Sp. Inf.* 192.			
	Dentalis. - - - - - - - 198.			
PYRALIS.	Koenigiana. - - - - - - 65.			
TINEA.	Cryptella. - - - - - - 25.			

ORDO VII. RYNGOTA.

FULGORA.	Diadema. L. *Fab. Sp. Inf.* N° 3.	*Seb. Muf.* - -		4. *t.* 77. *f.* 7. 8.
	Truncata. L. - - - - - 11.	*Amœn. Ac.* - -		6. *p.* 399. 40.
	Hyalinata. - - - - - - 12.			
	Festiva. - - - - - - - 13.			
MEMBRACIS.	Spinosa. - - - - - - - 5.	*Sulz. Inf.* - - - -		*t.* 9. *f.* 6.
	Taurus. - - - - - - - 10.			
TETTIGONIA.	Fornicata. - - *Gmel. Lin.* 11.	*Muf. Lud. Ulr.*		156.
	Fasciata. - - *Fab. Mantiss.* 2.	*Stoll. Cicad.* -		1. *t.* 4. *f.* 17.
	Spinosa. - - - - - - - 6.			
	Vaginata. - - - - - - - 7.			
	Conspurcata. - - *Sp. Inf.* 13.			
	Repanda. L. - - - - - - 16.	*De Geer, Inf.* -		3. *t.* 33. *f.* 1.
	Testacea. - - - *Mantiss.* 23.	*Stoll. Cicad.* -		1. *t.* 8. *f.* 41. C.

CICADA.

CICADA.	Perſpicillata.	*Fab. Sp. Inſ.* N°	1.		
	Ocellata.	- - - - - - -	2.	*De Geer, Inſ.* -	3. *t.* 33. *f.* 2.
	Cunicularia. L.	- - - - -	11.		
	Lanata. L.	- - - - - -	12.	*Drur. Inſ.* - -	2. *t.* 37. *f.* 11.
	Tomentoſa.	- - - - - -	13.		
	Barbata.	- - - - - - -	14.		
	Hyalina.	- - - - - -	31.		
	Lyncea.	- - - - - - -	37.		
NOTONECTA.	Nivea.	- - - - - - -	3.		
	Indica.	- - *Mantiſſ. p.*	534.		
NEPA.	Annulata.	- - - *Spec. Inſ.*	2.		
	Ruſtica.	- - - - - - -	3.		
	Fuſca.	- - - - *Mantiſſ.*	4.	*Stoll. Cimic.* - -	2. *t.* 1. *f.* 1.
	Rubra. L.	- - - - - - -	6.	- - - - - -	2. *t.* 7. V.
	Maculata.	- - *Sp. Inſ.* N°	6.		
	Linearis. L.	- - - - - -	7.	*Schæf. Icon.* - -	*t.* 5. *f.* 5. 6.
CIMEX.	Nobilis. L.	- - - - - -	2.	*Stoll. Cimic.* - -	1 *t.* 1. *f.* 1.
	Clavipes.	- - *Fab. Mantiſſ.*	5.		
	Maculatus.	- - - - - -	11.		
	Ruſticus.	- - - - - - -	26.		
	Lunatus.	- - - - *Sp. Inſ.*	9.	- - - - - -	2. *t.* 13. *f.* 84.
	Vahlii.	- - - - - - -	32.		
	Hiſtrio.	- - - *Gmel. Lin.*	12.		
	Grandis.	- - - - - - -	171.	*Thunb. N. Sp. Inſ.*	2. N° 31. *f.* 46.
	Taurus.	- - - - *Sp. Inſ.*	34.		
	Dentatus.	- - - - - -	43.		
	Spinidens.	- - - *Mantiſſ.*	61.		
	Hamatus.	- - - - - -	80.		
	Scaber.	- - - *Gmel. Lin.*	30.	*Amœn. Ac.* - -	6. *p.* 400. 43.
	Pugnator.	- *Fab. Mantiſſ.*	84.		

Thoracicus. - *Gmel. Lin.* 262. *Stoll. Cimic.* - - *t.* 8. *f.* 55. A.
Hastatus. - *Fab. Mantiss.* 88.
Analis. - - - *Gmel. Lin.* 263. - - - - - - - *t.* 10. *f.* 72. B.
Tenebrosus. - *Fab. Mantiss.* 93.
Sulcatus. - - *Gmel. Lin.* 271. - - - - - - - *t.* 6. *f.* 47.
Fulvicornis. - *Fab. Mantiss.* 94.
Pustulatus. - - *Gmel. Lin.* 281. *De Geer, Inf.* - 3. *t.* 34. *f.* 2.
Femoratus. - *Fab. Sp. Inf.* 77.
Aurantius. - - *Mantiss.* 116. *Stoll. Cim.* - - 1. *t.* 6. *f.* 39.
Punctum. - - - - - - 117. - - - - - - 2. *t.* 6. *f.* 40.
Nigripes. - - - *Sp. Inf.* 92. *Drur. Inf.* - - 2. *t.* 36. *f.* 5.
Torquatus. - - - - - - 93.
Guttatus. - - - *Mantiss.* 121.
Viridulus. L. - - *Sp. Inf.* 95. *Mus. Lud. Ulr.* 172.
Peregrinator. - *Gmel. Lin.* 40. - - - - - 173.
Beryllus. - - - *Mantiss.* 127.
Javanicus. - - *Gmel. Lin.* 332. *Stoll. Cim.* - - - *t.* 11. *f.* 2.
6-punctatus. L. *Fab. Sp. Inf.* 105. *Mus. Lud. Ulr.* 175.
Brunneus. - - *Gmel. Lin.* 334.
Rubrofasciatus. *Fab. Mantiss.* 140.
Ruficornis. - - *Sp. Inf.* 114.
Gramineus. - - *Mantiss.* 161.
Histrio. - - - - - - 167.
Pictus. - - - *Sp. Inf.* 117.
Faber. - - - *Mantiss.* 181.
Cruciatus. - - *Sp. Inf.* 122.
Indus. L. - - - - - - 140. *Mus. Lud. Ulr.* 176.
Civilis. - - - *Mantiss.* 186.
Familiaris. - - - - 190.
Varicornis. - - - - - - 194.
Malabaricus. *Fab. Sp. Inf.* N° 147.
Koenigii. - - - - - - - 156. *Stoll. Cimic.* - - 2. *t.* 1. *f.* 5.
Mendicus. - - - - - - 158.
Cruentus. - - *Mantiss.* 214.
Augur. - - - *Sp. Inf.* 167.

Mactans.

	Mactans. - - -	*Sp. Inf.*	168.		
	Erythrozonias. -	*Gmel. Lin.*	456.	*De Geer, Inf.* -	3. *t.* 35. *f.* 12.
	Sordidus. -	*Fab. Mantiff.*	231.		
	Calens. L. - -	*Sp. Inf.*	213.	*Gronov. Zooph.*	712.
	Gronovii. L. - - - - -		214.	- - - -	711.
	Cingulatus. - -	*Mantiff.*	287.		
	Pedeftris. - - -	*Sp. Inf.*	224.		
	Foffarum. - - - - - -		226.		
	Filum. - - - - - -		232.	*De Geer, Inf.* -	3. *t.* 35. *f.* 16.
Reduvius.	Gigas. - - - - - - - -		1.		
	Marginatus. - - - - - -		7.		
	Sanctus. - - -	*Mantiff.*	12.		
	Pilicornis. - - - - - -		19.		
	Collaris. - - -	*Sp. Inf.*	15.		
	Sexguttatus. - - - - - -		17.		
	4-guttatus. - - - - - -		18.		
	Aurantius. - - - - - - - -				
	Punctum. - - - - - - -		19.		
	Bipunctatus.	*Fab. Mantiff.*	N° 30.		
	Fufcipes. - - - - - - -		33.		
	5-fpinofus. - - -	*Sp. Inf.*	27.		

ORDO VIII. Antliata.

Bibio.	Lar. - - - - - - - -		10.
	Sphinx. - - -	*Mantiff.*	20.
	Troglodyta. - -	*Sp. Inf.*	20.
Syrphus.	Craffus. - - - -	*Mantiff.*	7.
	4-lineatus. - - - - - -		24.

MUSCA.	Jejuna. - - - - - - - - - 2.		
ASILUS.	Maculatus. - - - *Sp. Inf.* 21.		
MYOPA.	Cincta. - - - - - - - - - 4.		
BOMBYLIUS.	Maculatus. - - - - - - 7.		
PEDICULUS.	Humanus. L. - - - - - 1.	*Schæf. Elem.* - -	*t.* 95.
	Pubis. L. - - - - - - - - 2.	*Red. Exper.* - -	*t.* 19. *f.* 1.
	Vulturis. - - - - - - - 4.		
ACARUS.	Elephantinus. L. *Fab. Sp. Inf.* N° 1.	*Schrank. Beytr.* -	*t.* 6. *f.* 14. 15.
	Indus. L. - - - - - - 12.		

CLASS

CLASS VI. VERMES.

I. INTESTINA.

N. B. From our ignorance of the productions of *India* in this Class, we are obliged to omit many Genera.

GORDIUS. MEdinensis. - - - - *Sloane Jam.* ii. 190. *tab.* 233. *fig.* 1.

SIPUNCULUS. Saccatus. - - - - - - - - - *Amœn. Acad.* iv. 454. *tab.* 3.

II. MOLLUSCA.

DORIS. Verrucosa. - - - - - - - - - *Seb. Mus.* ii. *tab.* 61. *fig.* 5.

NEREIS. Noctiluca. - - - - - - - - *Amœn. Acad.* iii. 203. *tab.* 3.
Gigantea. - - - - - - - - - - *Seb. Mus.* i. *tab.* 81. *fig.* 7.

ACTINIA. Swalloo. - - - An edible Species collected in the *Molucca Isles.*

HOLUTHURIA. Priapus. - - - - - - - - - - - - *Amœn. Acad.* iv. 255.

SEPIA. Octopodia. *Br. Zool.* iv. N° 44. *tab.* 28. Of a monstrous size in *India.*

MEDUSA. Porpita. - - - - - *Amœn. Acad.* iv. 255. *tab.* 3. *fig.* 7. 8.

* ENTIRE.

* ENTIRE.

ASTERIAS. Luna. - - - - - - - - *Amœn. Acad.* iv. 256. *tab.* 3. *fig.* 14.

** STELLATED.

Reticulata. - - - - - *Linck. tab.* 41. *fig.* 72. *tab.* 23. *fig.* 36.
Nodosa. - - - - - - - - - - - *Seb. Mus.* iii. *tab.* 5. *fig.* 7. 8.
Lævigata. - - - - - - - - - - *Grew. Mus. tab.* 8. *fig.* 1. 2.

*** RADIATED.

Ciliaris. - - - - - - - - *Linck. tab.* 40. *fig.* 70. *tab.* 37. & 56.
Pectinata. - - - - - - - - - - - *Linck. tab.* 37. *fig.* 64. 66.
Multiradiata. - - - - - - - - - - *Linck. tab.* 21. *fig.* 33.
Caput Medusæ. *Seb. Mus.* iii. *tab.* 9. & *tab.* 11. *Rumph. Mus.* 41. *tab.* 16.

ECHINUS. Esculentus. - - - - - - - - - *Rumph. Mus.* 31. *tab.* 13. B.
Globulus. - - - - - - - - - - - - - - *M. L. U.* 706.
Sphæroides.
Gratilla. - - - - - - - - - - - - - - *M. L. U.* 707.
Lixula. - - - - - - - - - - - - - - - - *Ibid.*
Diadema. - - - - - - - - - - - *Rumph. Mus. tab.* 14. B.
Lucunter. - - - - - - - - - - *Gualt. Test. tab.* 107. *fig.* C.
Atratus. - - - - - - - - - - *Rumph. Mus.* iii. *tab.* 13. *fig.* 2.
Lacunatus. - - - - - - - - - - - - *Ibid. tab.* 14. *fig.* 2.
Rosaceus. - - - - - - - - - - *Rumph. Mus. tab.* 14. *fig.* 2.
Orbiculus. δ. - - - - - - - - - - - *Gualt. tab.* 7. *fig.* B.

III. Testacea:

DIV. I. Multivalvia.

Chiton.	Aculeatus.	*Rumph. Muſ. tab.* 10. *fig.* 4.
	Squammoſus.	*M. L. U.* 465 *.
	Punctatus.	*Seb. Muſ.* iii. *tab.* 1. *fig.* 13.
Lepas.	Diadema.	*Rumph. Muſ. tab.* 14. *fig.* H.
	Anatifera.	*Argenville, tab.* 26. *fig.* F. G.
	Teſtudinaria.	*Rumph. Muſ. tab.* 40. *fig.* K.

Pholas. Dactylus, Born. 14. I muſt not omit my acknowlegements to the magnificent work on Shells by the *Chevalier Ignatius a Born*, for very conſiderable additions to this Catalogue. Rumphius, juſtly ſtyled the Pliny, muſt have the preference in every authority, as the great collector of moſt of the articles referred to.

DIV. II. Bivalvia.

Mya.	Vulſella.	*Rumph. Muſ. tab.* 90. *fig.* H.

Solen.

SOLEN.	Vagina.	*Rumph. Muf. tab.* 45. *fig.* M.
	Cultellus.	*Ibid. fig.* F.
	Radiatus.	*Ibid. fig.* E.
	Anatinus.	*Ibid. fig.* O.
	Bullatus.	*Ibid. tab.* 44. *fig.* N.
	Virens.	

* OVATÆ.

TELLINA.	Gargadia.	*Rumph. Muf. tab.* 43. *fig.* N.
	Lingua Felis.	*tab.* 45. *fig.* G.
	Virgata.	*tab.* 45. *fig.* H.
	Angulata.	*Lift. Conch. tab.* 394. *fig.* 241.
	Gari.	*tab.* 45. *fig.* D.
	Foliacea.	*tab.* 45. *fig.* K.
	Lævigata.	*tab.* 45. *fig.* I.
	Roftrata.	*Argenville, tab.* 22. *fig.* O.
	Truncata.	

** SUBORBICULATÆ.

	Remies.	*Rumph. Muf. tab.* 43. *fig.* 1.
	Reticulata.	*fig.* E.
	Scobinata.	*Gualt. tab.* 76. *fig.* E.

CARDIUM.	Cardiffa.	*Rumph. Muf. tab.* 42. *fig.* E.
	Retufum.	*Born.* 41. *tab.* 111. *fig.* 1. 2.
	Hemicardium.	*tab.* 44. *fig.* H.
	Medium.	*M. L. U.* 485. N° 34.
	Tuberculatum.	*Rumph. Muf. tab.* 48. *fig.* 11.
	Fragum.	*tab.* 44. *fig.* G.
	Unedo.	*tab.* 44. *fig.* F.
	Ifocardia.	*tab.* 48. *fig.* 9.

Æolicum.

	Æolicum. - - - - - - - - - - - -	*Bonan.* ii. *fig.* 91.
	Rusticum. - - - - - - - - -	*Rumph. Muf. tab.* 44. *fig.* K.
MACTRA.	Plicataria.	
	Sprengleri. - - - - - - - - - - -	*Gualt. tab.* 85. *fig.* F.
	Trunculus. - - - - - - - - - -	*Bonan.* lv. *tab.* 4. *fig.* 3. 4.
	Scortum. - - - - - - - - - - -	*Argenville, tab.* 21. *fig.* L.
DONAX.	Pubescens. - - - - - - - - - -	*M. L. U.* 493. N° 49 *.
	Trunculus. - - - - - - - - -	BORN. lv. *tab.* iv. *fig.* 3. 4.
	Scortum. - - - - - - - - - - - - -	liii. *tab.* iv. *fig.* 1.
VENUS.	Gallina. - - - - - - - - - - - - -	*Bonan.* ii. *tab.* 64. 65.
	Flexuofa. - - - - - - - - - - -	*Rumph. Muf. tab.* 43. *fig.* O.
	Chione. - - - - - - - - - - - - - - -	*tab.* 42. *fig.* 9.
	Meretrix. - - - - - - - - - - - - -	*Argenv. tab.* 21. *fig.* F.
	Læta. - - - - - - - - - - - - - -	*Gualt. tab.* 28. *fig.* V.
	Castrensis. - - - - - - - - - - -	*Rumph. Muf. tab.* 42. *fig.* K.
	Fimbriata. - - - - - - - - - - - - - -	*tab.* 43. *fig.* F.
	Squammofa. - - - - - - - - - - - - -	*tab.* 44. *fig.* M.

*** IMPUBERES ORBICULATÆ.

Tigerina. - - - - - - - - - - - - - -	*tab.* 43. *fig.* H.
Prostrata. - - - - - - - - - - - -	*M. L. U.* 504. N° 66 *.
Incrustata. - - - - - - - - - -	*List. Conch tab.* 310. *fig.* 146.
Tigerina Secunda. - - - - - -	*Rumph. Muf. tab.* 43. *fig.* H.
Pectinata. - - - - - - - - - - - - - -	*tab.* 42. *fig.* D.
Scripta. - - - - - - - - - - - - - -	*tab.* 43. *fig.* C.
Edentula. - - - - - - - - - - - -	*M. L. U.* 508. N° 74 *.
Punctata. - - - - - - - - - - -	*Rumph. Muf. tab.* 43. *fig.* G.

**** IMPUBERES OVALES, SUPRA RIMAM SUBANGULATÆ.

	Litterata.	*Rumph. Muf. tab.* 43. *fig.* B.
	Rotundata.	*M. L. U.* 509. N° 76 *.
	Decuffata.	*M. L. U.* 509. N° 77.
	Virginea.	
SPONDYLUS.	Regius.	*Rumph. Muf.* 156. N° 8.
	Plicatus.	*tab.* 47. *Oftrea Electrica.*
	Gæderopus.	*tab.* 47. *fig.* E. 48. *fig.* 1. 2.
CHAMA.	Gigas.	*tab.* 43. *fig.* A. B.
	Hippopus.	*tab.* 42. *fig.* C.
	Lazarus.	BORN. 83. *tab.* 5. *fig.* 12. 13. 14.
	Arcinella.	BORN. *Davila, tab.* 27. *fig.* T.
	Gryphoides.	*Bonan.* ii. *fig.* 22.

* MARGINE INTEGERRIMO, NARIBUS RECURVATIS.

ARCA.	Noæ.	*tab.* 44. *fig.* P.

** MARGINE CRENATO.

Antiquata.	*tab.* 44. *fig.* I.
Decuffata.	*Bonan.* ii. *fig.* 60.
Pallens.	*M. L. U.* 520. N° 95.
Tortuofa.	*Rumph. Muf. tab.* 47. *fig.* K.
Rhombea.	*Lift. Conch. tab.* 244. *fig.* 75.
Pectunculus.	*tab.* 239. *fig.* 73.

* PECTINES

* Pectines Auriculati, Æquilateres.

Ostrea.	Striatula. - - - - - - - - - - -	*M. L. U.* 523. N° 101.
	Minuta. - - - - - - - - - - - - - - -	524. N° 102.
	Pleuronectes. - - - - - - -	*Rumph. Muf. tab.* 45. *fig.* A. B.
	Radula. - - - - - - - - - - - - - -	*tab.* 44. *fig.* A.
	Plica. - - - - - - - - - - - - - - -	*tab.* 44. *fig.* O.

** Pectines Auricula altera intus Ciliato-Spinosa.

	Pallium. - - - - - - - - - - - - -	*tab.* 44. *fig.* B. C.
	Nodofa. - - - - - - - - - - - - - -	*tab.* 48. *fig.* B.
	Lima. - - - - - - - - - - - - - - -	*tab.* 44. *fig.* D.
	Cucullata. - - . - - - - -	*Born.* 114. *tab.* vi. *fig.* 11. 12.

*** Rudes, Ostreæ dictæ.

	Malleus. - - - - - - - - - -	*Rumph. Muf. tab.* 47. *fig.* H.
	Edulis.? - - - - - - - - - - - - -	*Bonan.* 108. *tab.* 70.
	Perna.	
	Ifogonum. - - - - - - - - - - -	*Gualt. tab.* 97. *fig.* A.
	Ephippium. - - - - - - - - -	*Rumph. Muf. tab.* 47. *fig.* B.
Anomia.	Placenta. -	*Lifter Conch. tab.* 104. *fig.* B. *Seb. Muf.* iii. *tab.* 90. *fig.* 8. 9.

** Parasitici, Unguibus affixi.

Mytilus.	Crifta Galli. - - - - - - - - - - - - -	*tab.* 47. *fig.* D.
	Frons. - - - - - - - - - - -	*Argenville, tab.* 19. *fig.* D.

** Plani Compressi.

Margariteferus. - - - - - - - *Rumph. Muſ. tab.* 40. *fig.* F.

*** Ventricosiusculi.

Lithophagus. - - - - - - - - - - - - - *tab.* 46. *fig.* F.
Bilocularis. - - - - - - - - - - - - *M. L. U.* 540. N° 133.
Edulis. - - - - - - - - - - - - *Liſt. Ang.* 182. *fig.* 28.
Pictus. - - - - - - - - - - - - *Born.* 127. *tab.* vii. *fig.* 6. 7.
Modiolus. - - - - - - - - - - *Rumph. Muſ. tab.* 46. *fig.* B.

Pinna. Rudis. - - - - - - - - - - - - - - - - - *tab.* 46. *fig.* L.
Pectinata. - - - - - - - - - - - - - *Gualt. tab.* 79. *fig.* A.
Saccata. - - - - - - - - - - - *Rumph. Muſ. tab.* 46. *fig.* N.
Digitiformis. - - - - - - - - - - - *M. L. U.* 546. N° 146.
Lobata. - - - - - - - - - - - - - - - - - 547. N° 147.
Incurvata. - - - - - - - - *Born. Rumph. Muſ. tab.* 46. *fig.* M.
Muricata. - - - - - - - - - - *Rumph. Muſ. tab.* 46. *fig.* M.

DIV. III. Turbinata.

Argonauta. Argo. - - - - - - - - - - *Rumph. Muſ. tab.* 18. *fig.* A. B.

Nautilus.

NAUTILUS.	Pompilius.	*Rumph. Muf. tab.* 17. *fig.* A. C. D.
	Spirula.	*tab.* 20. *fig.* 1.
CONUS.	Marmoreus.	*tab.* 32. *fig.* N. I.
	Imperialis.	*tab.* 34. *fig.* H. I.
	Literatus.	*tab.* 31. *fig.* D.
	Generalis.	*tab.* 33. *fig.* V.
	Virgo.	*tab.* 31. *fig.* I. K.
	Capitaneus.	*tab.* 33. *fig.* K.
	Miles.	*tab.* 33. *fig.* W.

** SPIRA PYRAMIDATA.

	Summus Admiralis.	*tab.* 34. *fig.* B. C. D.
	Ebæus.	*tab.* 32. *fig.* B. B.
	Glaucus.	*tab.* 33. *fig.* G. G.
	Monachus.	*tab.* 33. *fig.* C. C.
	Minimus.	*Argenville, tab.* 12. *fig.* A.
	Betulinus.	*Rumph. Muf. tab.* 31. *fig.* C.
	Stercus Mufcarum.	*tab.* 33. *fig.* 3. A. A.
	Nuffatella.	*tab.* 33. *fig.* E. E.
	Textile.	*tab.* 32. *fig.* O. P.
	Aulicus.	*tab.* 33. *fig.* 3.
	Striatus.	*tab.* 31. *fig.* F.
	Magus.	*tab.* 32. *fig.* 2.
	Tragulinus.	*tab.* 31. *fig.* V.
	Ermineus.	*Seb. Muf.* iii. *tab.* 42. *fig.* 31. 34. 35. 40.
	Varius.	*Argenville, tab.* 12. *fig.* R.
	Spectrum.	*Rumph. Muf. tab.* 32. *fig.* 1.
	Tulipa.	*tab.* 34. *fig.* K. L.
	Geographus.	*tab.* 31. *fig.* G.
CYPRÆA.	Mappa.	*tab.* 38. *fig.* B.

Arabica.

	Arabica.	*Rumph. Muſ. tab.* 38. *fig.* M.
	Carneola.	*tab.* 38. *fig.* K.
	Teſtudinaria.	*tab.* 38. *fig.* C.
	Talpa.	*tab.* 38. *fig.* I.
	Caput Serpentis.	*tab.* 38. *fig.* F.
	Mauritiana.	*tab.* 38. *fig.* E.
	Vitellus.	*tab.* 38. *fig.* L.
	Tigris.	*tab.* 38. *fig.* A.
	Lynx.	*Liſter Conch. tab.* 683. *fig.* 30.
	Iſabella.	*Rumph. Muſ. tab.* 39. *fig.* G.
	Onyx.	*tab.* 38. *fig.* B.
	Hirundo.	*Liſter Conch. tab.* 674. *fig.* 20. *Born.* 184. *tab.* viii. *fig.* 11.
	Aſellus.	*Rumph. Muſ. tab.* 39. *fig.* M.
	Cribraria.	*Liſter Conch. tab.* 695. *fig.* 42.
	Moneta.	*Rumph. Muſ. tab.* 39. *fig.* C.
	Annulus.	*tab.* 39. *fig.* D.
	Caurica.	*tab.* 38. *fig.* P.
	Dracæna.	*tab.* 39. *fig.* E.
	Eroſa.	*tab.* 39. *fig.* A.
	Helvola.	*tab.* 16. *fig.* 17.
	Ocellata.	*Liſter Conch. tab.* 696. *fig.* 43.
	Pediculus.	*Rumph. Muſ. tab.* 39. *fig.* P.
	Nucleus.	*tab.* 39. *fig.* I.
	Staphylæa.	*Born.* 194. *tab.* viii. *fig.* 18.
	Cicercula.	*Rumph. Muſ. tab.* 39. *fig.* K.
	Globulus.	*tab.* 39. *fig.* N.
BULLA.	Ovum.	*tab.* 38. *fig.* Q.
	Biroſtris.	*Liſter Conch. tab.* 711. *fig.* 66.
	Verrucoſa.	*Rumph. Muſ. tab.* 38. *fig.* H.
	Naucum.	*tab.* 27. *fig.* H.
	Ampulla.	*tab.* 27. *fig.* G.
	Phyſis.	*Liſter Conch. tab.* 715. *fig.* 75.
	Ampluſtre.	*Born. tab.* ix. *fig.* 1.
	Ficus.	*Rumph. Muſ. tab.* 27. *fig.* K.

	Rapa.	*Rumph. Muf. tab.* 27. *fig.* E.
	Terebellum.	*tab.* 36. *fig.* S.
	Virginea.	*Lifter Conch. tab.* 12. *fig.* 7. *tab.* 15. *fig.* 10.
	Achatina.	*Born. tab.* x. *fig.* 1. 2.
VOLUTA.	Auris Midæ.	*Rumph. Muf. tab.* 33. *fig.* H. H.
	Oliva.	*tab.* 39. *fig.* 3.
	Et Plurimæ Variet.	Vide *Born.* 214. 215.
	Gibbofa.?	*Lifter Conch. tab.* 723. *fig.* 10.
	Hifpidula.	*Born.* γ. *Lift. Conch. tab.* 722. *fig.* 9.
	Bullata.	*tab.* 83. *fig.* 11.
	Dactylus.	*tab.* 812. *fig.* 23.
	Scabricula.	*Gualt. tab.* 53. *fig.* D.
	Sanguifuga.	*Rumph. Muf. tab.* 29. *fig.* V.
	Caffra.	*Gualt. tab.* 53. *fig.* E.
	Vulpecula.	*Rumph. Muf. tab.* 29. *fig.* R.
	Plicaria.	*Gualt. tab.* 54. *fig.* F.
	Epifcopalis.	*Rumph. Muf. tab.* 29. *fig.* K.
	Mitra Papalis.	*tab.* 29. *fig.* I.
	Capitellum.	*Gualt. tab.* 37. *fig.* A.
	Muricata.	*Martin Konch.* iii. *tab.* 99.
	Ceramica.	*Rumph. Muf. tab.* 24. *fig.* A. *tab.* 49. *fig.* L.
	Pyrum.	*tab.* 36. *fig.* 7.
	Æthiopica.	*tab.* 31. *fig.* B. A.
	Olla.	*Gualter. tab.* 29. *fig.* A.

* AMPULLACEÆ.

BUCCINUM.	Galea.	*Rondel. Teft. p.* 106.
	Perdix.	*Rumph. Muf. tab.* 27. *fig.* C.
	Pomum.	*tab.* 27. *fig.* B.
	Sulcofum.	*Seb. Muf.* iii. *tab.* 68 *fig.* 14. 15.
	Dolium.	*Rumph. Muf. tab.* 27. *fig.* A.

** CASSIDEA.

** CASSIDEA.

Echinophorum. - - - - - - - - *Rumph. Mus. tab.* 27. *fig.* 1.
Cornutum. - - - - - - - - - - - - - - *tab.* 23. *fig.* 1.
Rufum. - - - - - - - - - - - - - - - *tab.* 23. *fig.* B.
Tuberosum. - - - - - - - *Seb. Mus.* iii. *tab.* 73. *fig.* 10. 11.
Flammeum. - - - - - - - - - *Rumph. Mus. tab.* 23. *fig.* 2.
Pullus. - - - - - - - - - - - - - - - *tab.* 23. *fig.* C.
Areola. - - - - - - - - - - - - - - *tab.* 25. *fig.* B. & 1.
Granulatum. - - - - - - - - - - - - - *tab.* 25. *fig.* C.

*** CASSIDEA LABRO MURICATO.

Erinaceus. - - - - - - - - - - - - - *tab.* 25. *fig.* D. 6. 7.
Glaucum. - - - - - - - - - - - - - - *tab.* 25. *fig.* A.
Vibex. - - - - - - - - - - - - - - - *tab.* 25. *fig.* E.
Papillosum. - - - - - - - - - - - - - *tab.* 29. *fig.* M.
Glans. - - - - - - - - - - - - - - - *tab.* 29. *fig.* P.

**** CALLOSA AD COLUM. REFLEXAM.

Arcularia. - - - - - - - - - - - - - - *tab.* 27. *fig.* M.

***** COLUM. QUASI ABROSA, PLANA.

Harpa. - - - - - - - - - - - - - - - *tab.* 32. *fig.* K. L.
Persicum. - - - - - - - - - - - - - - *tab.* 27. *fig.* E.
Smaragdulus. - - - - - - - - - *Argenville, tab.* 6. *fig.* P.

****** GLABRA.

****** GLABRA.

Spiratum. - - - - - - - - - *Rumph. Muf. tab.* 49. *fig.* C. D.
Glabratum. - - - - - - - - - - - *Argenville. tab.* 9. *fig.* G.

******* ANGULATA.

Undofum. - - - - - - - - - - *Rumph. Muf. tab.* 29. *fig.* O.
Bezoar. - - - - - - - - - - - - *Argenville, tab.* 15. *fig.* G.

******** TURRITA, LÆVIA, SUBULATA.

Maculatum. - - - - - - - - - *Rumph. Muf. tab.* 30. *fig.* A.
Subulatum. - - - - - - - - - - - - - - - *tab.* 30. *fig.* B.
Crenulatum. - - - - - - - - - - - - - *tab.* 30. *fig.* E.
Strigilatum. - - - - - - - - - - - - - - *tab.* 30. *fig.* H.
Duplicatum. - - - - - - - - - - - - *Bonan.* iii. *fig.* 110.
Lanceatum. - - - - - - - - - - *Rumph. Muf. tab.* 30. *fig.* O.
Dimidiatum. - - - - - - - - - - - - - - *tab.* 30. *fig.* C.

* DIGITATI.

STROMBUS. Chiragra. - - - - - - - - - - - - - - *tab.* 35. *fig.* A. B.
Scorpius. - - - - - - - - - - - - - - - - *tab.* 36. *fig.* K.
Lambis. - - - - - - - - - - - - - - - *tab.* 35. *fig.* E. F. H.
Millepeda. - - - - - - - - - - - - - - - *tab.* 36. *fig.* I.

** LABRO LOBATO.

Lentiginofus. - - - - - - - - - - - - - - *tab.* 37. *fig.* Q.
Gallus. - - - - - - - - - - - - - - - - - *tab.* 37. *fig.* 5.

	Auris Dianæ. - - - - - - -	*Rumph. Muf. tab.* 37. *fig.* R.
	Luhuanus. - - - - - - - - - - - - -	*tab.* 37. *fig.* S.
	Gibberulus. - - - - - - - - - - - - -	*tab.* 37. *fig.* V.

*** LABRO AMPLIATO.

	Epidromis. - - - - - - - - - - - - -	*tab.* 36. *fig.* M.
	Canarium. - - - - - - - - - - - - -	*tab.* 36. *fig.* N.
	Vittatus. - - - - - - - - - - - - - -	*tab.* 37. *fig.* X.
	Urceus. - - - - - - - - - - - - - -	*tab.* 37. *fig.* T.

* SPINOSI.

MUREX.	Hauftellum. - - - - - - - - - - - - -	*tab.* 26. *fig.* E.
	Tribulus. - - - - - - - - - - - - - -	*tab.* 26. *fig.* G.
	Cornutus. - - - - - - - - - - - - -	*tab.* 26. *fig.* 5.
	Brandaris. - - - - - - - - - - - - -	*tab.* 26. *fig.* 4.

** FRONDOSI.

	Tripterus. - - - - - -	*Martin Konch.* iii. *tab.* 111. *fig.* 1033.
	Triqueter. - - - - - - - - - - - - - - -	*fig.* 1038.
	Ramofus. - - - - - - - - -	*Rumph. Muf. tab.* 26. *fig.* D.
	Saxatilis. - - - - - - - - - - - - - -	*tab.* 26. *fig.* C. a.

*** VARICOSI.

	Rana. - - - - - - - - - - - - - - -	*tab.* 26. *fig.* G. *et.*
	Varietas. - - - - - - - - - -	*Lifter Conch. tab.* 949. *fig.* 44.
	Lampas. - - - - - - - - - -	*Rumph. Muf. tab.* 28. *fig.* C.
	Olearium. - - - - - - - - - - - - -	*Bonan.* iii. *fig.* 289.
	Femorale. - - - - - - - - - -	*Rumph. Muf. tab.* 26. *fig.* B.

Pyrum.

Pyrum. - - - - - - - - - - - - *Rumph. Muf. tab.* 26. *fig.* E.
Rubecula. - - - - - - - - - - - - - - *Gualt. tab.* 49. *fig.* 1.
Anus. - - - - - - - - - - - - - *Rumph. Muf. tab.* 24. *fig.* F.

**** Echinati sine Rostro.

Hippocaftarum. - - - - - - - - - - - - - - *tab.* 24. *fig.* 4.
Mancinella. - - - - - - - - - - - - - - - *tab.* 24. *fig.* 5.
Ricinus. - - - - - - - - - - - - - - - - *tab.* 24. *fig.* E.
Senticofus. - - - - - - - - - - - - - - *tab.* 29. *fig.* N.
Melongena. - - - - - - - - - - - - - - - *tab.* 24. *fig.* E.
Rapiformis. - - - - - - - - - - *Lifter Conch. tab.* 894. *fig.* 14.
Lacerus. - - - - - - - - - - - - - - *Idem. tab.* 958. *fig.* 11.

***** Inermes Rostro Elongato.

Babylonius - - - - - - - - - - - *Rumph. Muf. tab.* 29. *fig.* L.
Javanus. - - - - - - - - - - - - - - - *Bonan.* iii. *fig.* 79.
Colus. - - - - - - - - - - - - - - *Rumph. Muf. tab.* 29. *fig.* F.
Morio. - - - - - - - - - - - - - - - *Bonan.* iii. *fig.* 357.
Cochlidium. - - - - - - - - - - - - *Argenville, tab.* 9. *fig.* A.
Spirillus. - - - - - - - - - - *Martin Konch. tab.* 115. *fig.* 1069.
Aruanus. - - - - - - - - - - - - *Rumph. Muf. tab.* 28. *fig.* A.
Tritonis. - - - - - - - - - - - - - - - - *tab.* 28. *fig.* B.

****** Turriti Subulati Rostro Brevi.

Vertagus. - - - - - - - - - - - - - - - - *tab.* 30. *fig.* K.
Sulcatus. - - - - - - - - - - - - - - - *Bonan.* iii. *fig.* 68.
Aluco. - - - - - - - - - - - - *Rumph. Muf. tab.* 30. *fig.* O.
Coronatus. - - - - - - - - - - - - - - - *tab.* 30. *fig.* N.
Radula. - - - - - - - - - - - - - - - *Bonan.* iii. *fig.* 327.

* UMBILICATI.

TROCHUS.	Niloticus.	*Rumph. Mus. tab.* 21. *fig.* A.
	Maculatus.	*tab.* 21. *fig.* c. *Bonan.* iii. *fig.* 27. 28.
	Perspectivus.	*tab.* 27. *fig.* L.
	Solaris.	*tab.* 20. *fig.* K.

** IMPERFORATI.

	Vestiarius.	*Lister Conch. tab.* 650.–51. *fig.* 46. 48.
	Labio.	*Rumph. Mus. tab.* 21. *fig.* E.

*** TURRITI.

	Telescopium.	*tab.* 21. *fig.* 12.

* SOLIDI, IMPERFORATI.

TURBO.	Cochlus.	*tab.* 19. *fig.* 4.
	Petholatus.	*tab.* 19. *fig.* D. 5. 6. 7.
	Chrysostomus.	*tab.* 19. *fig.* E.
	Pagodus.	*tab.* 21. *fig.* D.
	Calcar.	*tab.* 20. *fig.* I.
	Rugosus.	*Bonan.* iii. *fig.* 12.
	Marmoratus.	*Rumph. Mus. tab.* 19. *fig.* A. B.

** PERFORATI, SOLIDI.

	Pica.	*tab.* 21. *fig.* A.
	Argyrostomus.	*tab.* 19. *fig.* 3.
	Margaritaceus?	*Bonan.* iii. *fig.* 11.

Delphinus.

Delphinus. - - - - - - - - - - - - - - *Bonan.* iii. *fig.* 31.
Distortus. - - - - - - - - - - *Rumph. Muf. tab.* 20. *fig.* H.
Scalaris. Wentel-trap. - - - - - - - - - - *tab.* 49. *fig.* A.

* Testa Ancipiti.

Helix. Scarabeus. - - - - - - - - - - - - - - - *tab.* 27. *fig.* I.

** Anfractibus Carinatis.

Ringens. - - - - - - - - - - - - *Bonan.* iii. *fig.* 330. 331.
Carocolla. - - - - - - - - - - - *Argenville, tab.* 8. *fig.* D.

*** Umbilicatæ Anfractibus Rotundis.

Cornea. - - - - - - - - - *Br. Zool.* iv. *tab.* 83. *fig.* 126.
Ampullacea. - - - - - - - - *Rumph. Muf. tab.* 27. *fig.* Q.
Cretacea. - - - - - - - - - - - - *Born. tab.* xvi. *fig.* 1. 2.
Ungulina. - - - - - - - - - - *Rumph. Muf. tab.* 27. *fig.* R.
Janthina. - - - - - - - - - - - - - - - - *tab.* 20. *fig.* 2.

**** Ovatæ Imperforatæ.

Amarula. - - - - - - - - - - - - - - *tab.* 33. *fig.* F. F.
Haliotoidea. - - - - - - - - - - - - - - *tab.* 90. *fig.* R.

* Umbilicatæ.

Nerita. Canrena. - *Bonan.* iii. *fig.* 228. 224. et *Argenville, tab.* 7. *fig.* C.
Glaucina. - - - - - - - - - *Brit. Zool.* iv. *tab.* 87. *fig.* 141.
Rufa. - - - - - - - - - - *Rumph. Muf. tab.* 22. *fig.* D.

Vitellus.

	Vitellus.	*Rumph. Muf. tab.* 22. *fig.* A.
	Albumen.	*tab.* 22. *fig.* B.
	Mamilla.	*tab.* 22. *fig.* F.

** IMPERFORATÆ, EDENTUTÆ.

	Cornea.	*Argenville, tab.* 7. *fig.* M.

*** IMPERFORATÆ, DENTATÆ.

	Pulligera.	*Lifter Conch. tab.* 143. *fig.* 37.
	Pennata.	*tab.* 604. *fig.* 29.
	Polita. α.	*tab.* 600. *fig.* 7.
	* β.	*Bonan.* iii. *fig.* 221.
	γ.	*Rumph. Muf. tab.* 22. *fig.* I.
	Peloronta.	*tab.* 22. *fig.* K.
	Albicilla.	*tab,* 22. *fig.* 8.
	Groffa.	*tab.* 22. *fig.* N.
	Chamæleon.	*tab.* 22. *fig.* L.
	Undata.	*tab.* 22. *fig.* 4.
	Exuvia.	*tab.* 22. *fig.* 9.
HALIOTIS.	Midæ.	*Argenville, tab.* 3. *fig.* A.
	Striata.	*Martin Konch.* i. *tab.* 14. *fig.* 138.
	Marmorata.	*Argenville, tab.* 3. *fig.* B.
	Afinina.	*Rumph. Muf. tab.* 40. *fig.* E. F.

* LABIATÆ.

PATELLA.	Equeftris.	*tab.* 40. *fig.* P. O.

** ANGULATÆ.

** ANGULATÆ.

Saccharina. - - - - - - - - - - *Rumph. Muf. tab.* 40. *fig.* B.

*** MUCRONATÆ.

Lutea. - - - - - - - - - - - *Born.* 424. *tab.* 17. *fig.* 8.

**** INTEGERRIMÆ VERTICE OBTUSO.

Teftudinaria. - - - - - - - - - - *Argenville, tab.* 2. *fig.* P.
Radiata. - - - - - - - - - - - - *Born. tab.* 18. *fig.* 10.
Compreffa. - - - - - - - - - *Lifter Conch. tab.* 541. *fig.* 25.
Fufca. - - - - - - - - - - - - - - *Bonan.* i. *fig.* 4.

DENTALIUM. Elephantinum. - - - - - - - *Rumph. Muf. tab.* 41. *fig.* I.
Dentalis. - - - - - - - - - - - - - - - *tab.* 41. *fig.* C.
Entalis. - - - - - - - - - - - - - - - *Bonan.* i. *fig.* 9.
Politum. - - - - - - - - - - - - - *Gualt. tab.* 10. *fig.* F.
Aprinum. - - - - - - - - - - - - - LINNÆI.
Eburneum. - - - - - - - - - - - - LINNÆI.

SERPULA. Lumbricalis. - - - - - - - - *Rumph. Muf. tab.* 41. *fig.* 1.
Polythalamia. - - - - - - - - - - - - - *tab.* 41. *fig.* D. E.
Arenaria. - - - - - - - - - - - - - - - *tab.* 41. *fig.* L.
Anguina. - - - - - - - - - - - - - - - *tab.* 41. *fig.* 2.
Muricata. - - - - - - - - - - - - - - *tab.* 41. *fig.* H.
Penis. - - - - - - - - - - - - - - - - *tab.* 41. *fig.* 7.

TEREDO. Navalis. - - - - - - - - - - - *Planc. Conch.* 17. N° 2.

§ SABELLA.

SABELLA.	Scruposa. - - - - - - - - - - - - - - - -	LINNÆI.

IV. LITHOPHYTA.

TUBIPORA.	Musica. - - - - - - - - - - - - -	*Ellis Zooph. pag.* 144.
MADREPORA.	Fungites. - - - - - - - - - - - - - - - -	*pag.* 149.
	Pileus. - - - - - - - - - -	*Rumph. Amb.* vi. *t.* 88. *f.* 2. 3.
	Labyrinthiformis. - - - - - -	*Ellis Zooph. pag.* 160. N° 34.
	Favosa. - - - - - - - - - - - - - - -	*pag.* 167. N° 61.
	Polygama. - - - - - - - - -	*Amœn. Acad.* iv. *tab.* 3. *fig.* 15.
	Fascicularis. - - - - - - - - -	*Ellis Zooph. pag.* 151. N° 5.
	Porites. - - - - - - - - - - - - - - -	*pag.* 172. N° 77.
	Damicornis. - - - - - - - -	*Rumph. Amb.* vi. *tab.* 86. *fig.* 3.
	Muricata. - - - - - - - - - - -	*Ellis Zooph. pag.* 171. N° 76.
	Oculata. - - - - - - - - - - -	*Seb. Mus.* iii. *tab.* 116. *fig.* 1. 2.
	Infundibuliformis. - - - - - - - - - -	*Gualt. Test. tab.* 42.
	Fastigiata. - - - - - - - - - - -	*Ellis Zooph. pag.* 152. N° 8.
	Ascillaris. - - - - - - - - - - - - - - -	*pag.* 153. N° 11.
	Anthophyllites. - - - - - - - - - - - - -	*pag.* 151. N° 4.
	Cristata. - - - - - - - - - - - - - - -	*pag.* 158. N° 27.
	Aspera. - - - - - - - - - - - - - - - -	*pag.* 156. N° 21.
	Cinerascens. - - - - - - - - - - - - - -	*pag.* 157. N° 26.
	Dædalea. - - - - - - - - - - - - - - -	*pag.* 163. N° 43.
	Scabrosa. - - - - - - - - - - - - - - -	*pag.* 156. N° 22.
MILLEPORA.	Alcicornis. - - - - - - - - - -	*Sloan. Jam.* i. *tab.* 17. *fig.* 1.
	Fascialis. - - - - - - - - -	*Ellis Cor. tab.* 30. *fig.* A. a. b.
	Cellulosa. - - - - - - - - - - - - - -	*tab.* 25. *fig.* D. d.
	Polymorpha. - - - - - - - - - - - - -	*tab.* 27. *fig.* C.

V. ZOOPHYTA.

V. ZOOPHYTA.

ISIS.	Hippuris.	*Ellis Zooph. pag.* 105. N° 2.
	Ochracea.	*pag.* 105. N° 1.
GORGONIA.	Abies.	*pag.* 103. N° 6.
	β.	*pag.* 99. N° 1.
	Ænea.	*Rumph. Amb.* vi. *tab.* 80. *fig.* 2.
	Antipathes.	*tab.* 77.
	Pectinata.	*Ellis Zooph. pag.* 85. N° 9.
SPONGIA.	Flabelliformis.	*Rumph. Amb.* vi. *tab.* 80. *fig.* 1.
	Fistularis.	*Sloan. Jam.* i. *tab.* 24. *fig.* 1.
	Aculeata.	*Rumph. Amb.* vi. *tab.* 90. *fig.* 2.
	Tubulosa.	*Seb. Mus.* iii. *tab.* 97. *fig.* 2.
	Tomentosa.	*Ellis Zooph. pag.* 187. N° 7.
SERTULARIA.	Pennaria.	*Lin. Syst. pag.* 1313. N° 26.
	Pennatula.	*Ellis Zooph. pag.* 56. N° 31.
VORTICELLA.	Conglomerata.	*Amœn. Acad.* iv. *tab.* 3. *fig.* 1.

FINIS.